THE POLITICS OF DISAPPOINTMENT

CHATHAM HOUSE STUDIES IN POLITICAL THINKING
SERIES EDITOR: George J. Graham, Jr.
Vanderbilt University

THE POLITICS OF DISAPPOINTMENT

American Elections, 1976–94

Wilson Carey McWilliams

Rutgers, The State University of New Jersey

Chatham House Publishers, Inc.
Chatham, New Jersey

THE POLITICS OF DISAPPOINTMENT
American Elections, 1976–94

Chatham House Publishers, Inc.
Box One, Chatham, New Jersey 07928

Publisher: Edward Artinian
Editor: Christopher J. Kelaher
Production supervisor: Katharine F. Miller
Cover design: Lawrence Ratzkin
Composition: Bang, Motley, Olufsen
Printing and binding: R.R. Donnelley and Sons Company

LIBRARY OF CONGRESS CATALOGING-IN-PUBLICATION DATA

McWilliams, Wilson C.
    The politics of disappointment : American elections, 1976–94 /
Wilson Carey McWilliams.
        p.   cm. — (Chatham House studies in political thinking)
    Includes bibliographical references (p.   ) and index.
    ISBN 1-56643-028-3
        1. Elections—United States. 2. Presidents—United States—
Election. 3. United States. Congress—Elections, 1994. 4. United
States—Politics and government—1945–1989. 5. United States—
Politics and government—1989–   I. Title. II. Series.
JK1976.M39   1995
324.273′0929—dc20   95-18753
                                                                CIP

Manufactured in the United States of America
10   9   8   7   6   5   4   3   2   1

This book is for two exemplary political educators
who never missed a chance to cast a ballot,
my grandmother,
Harriet McWilliams (1874–1958),
a lifelong Republican in a family of Democrats, and
my mother,
Dorothy McWilliams (1905–72),
who voted for every Democrat from Al Smith
to George McGovern.

P80744

Contents

Preface

The accounts in this book appeared before or not too long after the elections they describe. In retrospect, my reflections and interpretations sometimes read pretty well, and sometimes they are very wrong. I have left them all as they were written, adding some footnotes where hindsight seems to require them, because my errors of judgment say at least as much about the problem of narrating elections as the instances where I get it right.

The treatments of the presidential elections of 1976–92 were originally printed in a series of volumes edited by my matchless colleague, Gerald M. Pomper. The first of these books, *The Election of 1976*, was published by David McKay; subsequent volumes were published by Chatham House; the entire series, along with this book, has been guided by Edward Artinian, as excellent an observer of politics and political science as he is a publisher. The three essays on the election of 1994 were written for *Commonweal*, from whose editors I have been receiving fine criticism and great generosity for what now comes to a third of a century.

I first wrote seriously about national elections as a junior co-author with my teacher, John H. Schaar, whose craft and wisdom and knowledge of things American are so remarkable that they rival his gift for friendship. Among many intellectual and personal debts, I am grateful to Dennis Bathory, Myron

Aronoff, Ross K. Baker, and my other colleagues at Rutgers University, to Dennis Hale and Marc Landy at Boston College, Bruce L. Payne at Duke University, and Nancy L. Schwartz at Wesleyan, to Henry Plotkin and Judge Florence Riley, and to three former and one current members of Congress—the late Allard Lowenstein, Don Pease, David Price, and Barney Frank —as well as to State Senator William Lockyer in California, for exemplifying honor in public office. And I owe the most important things—patience and prodding and joy among them—to my wife, Nancy, and my daughters, Helen and Susan, all great observers and grand partisans.

THE POLITICS OF DISAPPOINTMENT

Introduction

This book chronicles almost two decades of American elections marked by a politics of disappointment. In retrospect, Vietnam and Watergate, those symbols of disillusionment, seem only events in a much longer story. America, in the twenty years after World War II, had pains and oppressions to spare, but compared with our times, it also had a broader sphere of commonality, at least among whites, and a greater assurance that the future held something better. Otherwise very diverse Americans—conservatives such as Governor Kirk Fordice of Mississippi and neoliberals such as Mickey Kaus of the *New Republic*—treat the 1950s as a kind of standard; millions of others, unexpectedly, found themselves mourning Richard Nixon, a symbol of that decade who had preserved its style and tone like a beetle in amber.[1]

There have been good, even triumphant moments since, but most Americans, looking backward, are finding it hard not to see a long, slow slide: real wages declining, society deteriorating, gaps widening between old and young and rich and poor, the hopeful integrationism of the civil rights movement turned into a bitter politics of race. Even victory in the Cold War has resulted in international disorder, new threats, and few visible dividends.[2] Briefly, Carter, Bush, and Clinton roused hopes, and Ronald Reagan had a longer, more disastrous run, but all fell short of America's probably unrealizable expectations.

That experience has helped make Americans more distrustful of government, their leaders, and one another—a part of democracy's curriculum, but one that too many citizens are exaggerating into a whole.* Even so, the great majority of us—some wistful, some raging—yearn for a renewal of the promise of American life, and reflecting on the recent past may help us mark the new limits and possibilities of that old dream.

Elections are central to our kind of democracy and have come to be regarded, almost everywhere, as a sine qua non of any legitimate government. "Every people, big or small," Mikhail Gorbachev told Stephen Cohen, "should have free elections."[3] But according to Aristotle, the ancient Greeks associated elections with oligarchy or aristocracy, since elections presume that some are better qualified to rule than others. Democratic principles, by contrast, point toward selection by lot, since among equals, one is as good as another.[4] In that older view, democracy presumes citizens who share in rule, participating in sovereign deliberation if not by holding office. Democratic citizenship demands having a say, not merely a vote.

The American Framers, in contrast, while holding consent to be the foundation of just governance, despised ancient democracy as too weak and too turbulent.[5] Convinced that the mass of citizens were unqualified to rule, they regarded them as capable of calling rulers to account.† In the Framers' version of democracy, citizens act by choosing representatives; the few speak, the many vote.[6] Yet while their usage allows for our large-scale democratic republic, with its much-praised diversities, by emphasizing will at the expense of speech, it also entails a political problem.

Elections, constitutional forms, necessarily afford an "unfinished and distorted picture" of political life.[7] They record the preferences of voters but ignore their motives and reasons, reducing all voters to identical quantities and awarding victory to

---

* Clifford Orwin makes the democratic case for distrust, within limits, in "Democracy and Distrust: A Lesson from Thucydides," *American Scholar* 53 (1984): 313–25.

† Following, in this respect, Montesquieu's argument in *The Spirit of the Laws*, bk. 2, chap. 2.

the greatest number. Voting totals level the wise and the foolish, the passionate and the indifferent, just as they overlook differences of power. Even the equation of the majority with greater force, Locke argued, holds only in a state of nature where such distinctions, for the most part, have not made themselves felt. In civil society, majority rule is an artifice that depends on the goodwill—moral or interested—of strong and skilled minorities and hence on the self-restraint of the many.[8] Elections are at most the tip of the political iceberg. They simplify and organize opinion, and under ordinary circumstances they provide an unambiguous outcome, but at the price of obscuring the existential variety of political experience and opinion. In George V. Higgins's novel *Victories,* a retiring congressman, Henry Briggs, who is also a former major-league pitcher, remarks that, statistically, pitchers, like elected officials, get credit for a "win" that is made up of the efforts of a team.

> So how many victories are there in a game or an election? Probably, I think, as many as there are people who took part. So who knows what victories really are, then? What they mean, if they mean anything?[9]

George Higgins's feeling for democratic politics is as sure as his ear for dialogue. The meaning of an election lies in the relation between electoral quantities and human qualities, convention and nature. Elections, in other words, are occasions for narration, and the need to tell their stories rightly poses a decisive test for our political life and art.

In recent years, of course, American democracy has been hard pressed to get even a passing grade. Startlingly few potential voters make it to the polls, reflecting a long-term drift away from the ballot box; too many citizens pay little attention to politics and seem disposed to dismiss our institutions, cursorily, as inept or dominated by special interests.[10] For a multitude of Americans, the political story barely touches personal drama;

elections seem radically separated from the dilemmas and aspirations of everyday life.

Not that this is particularly surprising. Citizenship, after all, is an acquired taste or discipline. For the most part, people are drawn to politics by private motives, and only later develop public ones—"first by necessity," runs Tocqueville's axiom, "afterwards by choice."[11] Yet this progression presumes that first, we see our interests as crucially involved with politics and public policy, and second, that the experience of politics offers us something *beyond* interest—the dignity of being recognized and heard, the warmth of political friendship, and ultimately the possibility of noble deeds and the good life.[12] Yet all of this rests on the citizen's involvement with community and face-to-face associations, and the scale and complexity of our political life is systematically reducing the importance of local politics and personal participation.[13]

Formally, elections offer self-government; existentially, citizens encounter dependence and vulnerability, an exposure to organized power and technological changes—little understood and less subject to personal control—that are shattering and reshaping communities and relationships.[14] Citizens expect government to address these problems, but to be effective in taking on the forces of the time, government must *mirror* them, becoming caught up in the intricacies of technique and power. The result is a two-tier politics in which the world of the governing elites is increasingly removed from that of ordinary citizens. And it is only to be expected that numbers of those citizens will turn away, if only in a despairing assertion of dignity.

Moreover, that so many Americans rely so much on particular governmental policies encourages efforts to define such programs as "rights," subject to administrative and judicial authority but protected against majority opinion.[15] More and more politics, consequently, becomes extraelectoral, limiting the impact of votes and elections and contributing to frustration and disillusionment with the public aspects of democratic life.[16]

Even when government works, it reminds voters—and not

always subtly—of their dependence on it, so that any perceived failure is an invitation to indignation. The anger of Americans at government, however, is a mark of their need for it. Less government would not "empower" citizens, it would only leave them subject to the dominations and powers of the market, technology, and international society. By contrast, the results of the election of 1994 show that the public *has* power over government and in politics. But this very power makes government a target for resentment, especially in a liberal society historically suspicious of the public sector.[17]

Still, elections are at least a sort of catharsis, and the results in 1994 are an urgent argument for reforging the links between government and citizen. Historically, that chain has been best provided by party, but part of the story in these essays is the ongoing dilapidation of local party organizations and the broader but related problem of the parties' weakening hold on the electorate. With the ascendancy of the primary system and the declining ability of party organizations to filter candidates, the nominating process, and hence electoral choice, is more and more defined and determined by the media and by money.[18] In political calculations, cultivating elites counts for more, and developing personal relationships with ordinary voters for less: American politics, like the American economy, is becoming increasingly capital intensive rather than labor intensive.[19] The centralized, national bureaucracies of the major parties wax as their reserves of loyalty among voters wane. In rising numbers, Americans are wishing a plague on the houses of both parties.* This trend toward disaffiliation leaves a growing slice of the electorate politically unmoored, its opinions more volatile and open to influence, yet guarded and self-protective; campaigns are more important, more expensive, and more apt to be cast in essentially private terms.[20] Holding Democrats responsible for their discontents with Congress, the president, and government

---

* The signs have been evident for some time. See Jack Dennis, "Trends in Public Support for the American Party System," *British Journal of Political Science* 5 (1975): 187–230.

in general, voters in 1994 made a sort of bow in the direction of party government and accountability, but one that was largely negative, inarticulate, and without commitment.

I know that to many observers—Newt Gingrich is only the most strident—the election of 1994 was a portent, a clear indication that the "information revolution" is creating a new and vigorous civil society that allows for and demands the transfer of power from government to ordinary citizens. In its broadest form, this argument is simply silly. Advances in technology bring resources, but they do not democratize; new skills and sources of power may unsettle old elites, but they also create new ones, and the mass public gains a fair command of such new techniques only after they have been superseded.*

It seems likely that essentially abstract interactions in "virtual reality" will prove as inadequate as "virtual representation" did to Americans in 1776, and as incapable of eliciting deep allegiance. Effective political action calls for the aggregation of mass opinion, and while the new technologies make it possible to gather opinion more quickly and in greater volume than ever, they also make it more transient and reduce the likelihood that any individual opinion will receive serious consideration.† So far, moreover, the possibilities for interaction remain largely unrealized; associational "membership" solicited by direct mail or electronic communication comes down, pretty much, to the decision to contribute money, since for the most part, members do not deliberate about policy or even vote for officers. And while the "talk shows," elite managed, can mobilize rage, they cannot offer dignity; the sources of dignity and identity are local, like Tip O'Neill's politics. Any political renewal for American de-

---

* Hence Jacques Ellul's observation that technique is "inevitably undemocratic," in *The Technological Society* (New York: Vintage, 1964), 208; see, more generally, 208–18.

† Sidney Verba, "The Voice of the People," *PS* 26 (1993), 679. As Ellul writes, "American society is no longer in its youth, when propaganda consisted of one man speaking directly to other men." *The Technological Society*, 374.

mocracy will have to be founded on a "host of little democracies," the revitalization of local parties and civic life.²¹ Of course, such a rebirth is a long shot at best; what is certain is the passing of the old order.

A major thread connecting these essays is the emergence of what originally was called the "social issue," a debate over the shape and future of American culture rivaling class and economic policy as the preeminent basis of political conflict.²² Contemporary writers are apt to treat this "cultural politics" as something new, and so it is, in a sense. The election of 1972 was a portent: the great Democratic majority, already shaken by the conflict between "hawks" and "doves" over Vietnam (and foreign policy generally), was further divided by the alliance between George McGovern and the "counterculture," and today's Republicans are as eager to remind voters of that year as Democrats are to forget it.

On a broader view, the politics of culture is not a new story but part of an old one. American politics has always been shaped by the question of who and what is American. The relationship between culture and citizenship, like the tension between American ways and America's appeal to natural rights, has always been a quarrel more than a given. (It is worth remembering, in fact, that aliens were once allowed to vote in as many as twenty-two states.²³) And, at bottom, it is the argument between insiders and outsiders over the qualifications for full and dignified membership in the American polity that has shaped and reshaped our partisan lines of division.²⁴

Economic distinctions are a vital part of that history, of course, since economic inequality, especially the extreme disparity that exists in the United States, is a standing threat to political equality.²⁵ But in the voting booth, differences of wealth and class are potent to the extent that they are indices of dignity, touchstones of civic rank and membership.* Economic interests

---

* And, of course, economic and class distinctions are complicated and often overlapping. Norbert Wiley, "America's Unique Class Politics: the Interplay of Labor, Credit and Commodity Markets," *American So-*

alone will be decisive only when conditions seem overwhelming, as they did during the Great Depression or, in a much milder way, in 1992.[26] Even then, when we vote, our ideas about the direction of the economy as a whole are apt to outweigh our immediate circumstances. Political life is defined by our attachment to groups and to values more than by self-interest, narrowly defined, so "politics often resembles the world of religion more closely than the world of economics."[27]

For a century after the Civil War, American party politics was framed by the conflict that ranged a Republican Party that was predominantly Protestant, middle class, and northern against the Democrats' fractious coalition of outsiders, with its strength in the white South and the ethnic minorities of the North—the GAR's Main Street defending its America against a party rooted in "rum, Romanism and rebellion."* That cultural divide began to blur with the gradual reassimilation of the South and the slow acceptance of Catholics and other white ethnics, both processes edged along by the fading of memory and the increasing restiveness of African Americans. The signs of strain on the party system were visible in the 1920s, becoming full-blown with the politics of civil rights that succeeded World War II, and by 1960 the election of John Kennedy symbolized—though a lot of battles remained and remain to be fought—the transformation of the old America.[28] And that, pretty much, is where the first chapter of this book begins.

Now, the Solid South is a matter for historians, and among whites, ethnic distinctions, still potent here and there, are collapsing as social barriers. Precipitately, American political memory is becoming "vaguer and more fabulous." With a straight face, Newt Gingrich invokes Franklin Roosevelt, and Governor George Pataki (also confusing two Sumners, the radical Charles and the Social Darwinist, William Graham) finds inspiration for

ciological Review 32 (1967): 529–41.

    * The phrase, of course, is Rev. Samuel Borchard's famous description of the Democrats in 1884. Matthew Josephson, _The Politicos_ (New York: Harcourt, Brace, 1938), 369.

his effort to shrink government in Theodore Roosevelt, who
—as Mencken saw, closer to firsthand—favored "a paternalism
concerning itself with all things, from the regulation of coal-
mining and meat-packing to ... spelling and marital rights."[29]
And that rewriting of the past is, pretty much, an epitaph for
the old party politics.

Traditionally, the divisions of cultural politics loosely follow those of class; today, the two lines of conflict show some
tendency to diverge and often seem to be at odds.* In intellectual circles, the prevailing vision of cultural combat pits the
privileged order against the marginalized perspectives of race,
class, and gender. But in emphasis, and certainly in the media's
translation of this teaching, class gets short shrift: white European males and those who identify with them stand opposed to
women, racial minorities, and homosexuals, a distinction that
evidently cuts across class lines. And it does not help that contemporary cultural elites, devoted to fairly radical versions of
personal liberty, are at least suspicious of the repressive potential of the decencies; they take fewer pains than the economic
elite to disguise their contempt for the culture of the many, invit-
ing a resentment that makes the cultural divide unusually potent
in shaping political attitudes and affiliations.[30]

Our older cultural debates were conducted, for the most
part, in a decisively *public* language; challenges to the dominant
culture were cast in terms of the American creed, especially the
Declaration's proclamation of human equality.[31] That rhetoric,
with its appeal from convention to nature, still echoes in American political speech, but more and more contemporary argument—influenced by relativism and, most fashionably, by post-
modernism—is inclined to slight equality and commonality in
favor of the view that political identities and ideas reflect the
plural perspectives of groups, and particularly their relationship
to power. (This tendency is not confined to the left: Newt

---

   * Daniel Bell observed this separation of the cultural and economic spheres in *The Cultural Contradictions of Capitalism* (New York:
Basic Books, 1976).

Gingrich was forced to withdraw his nominee for House historian, Christina Price Jeffrey, after it was revealed that she had criticized a program on the Holocaust for failing to present the perspective of Nazis and Klansmen; such "unpopular" ideas, she argued, are "still a point of view," evincing a zeal for multicultural diversity that would make most of its advocates blanch.[32]) In an increasingly specialized society, where public spaces are threatened and public life is rare, any unraveling of political speech encourages the fragmentation of associations and parties and hence the ability of the "individually powerless many" to unite against the few.[33]

Two-party systems offer voters the clearest choice and the easiest means of holding government accountable, but they also presume that public opinion can be organized around some basic antithesis, some issue or concern perceived as sufficiently fundamental to unite those who stand on the same side and to override their differences. In that sense, all two-party politics is a single-issue politics that suppresses other divisions, the kind of conflict that sparks analogies between politics and war.[34]

On any given issue, two-party politics is natural, even inevitable, since every policy "implies a choice between two kinds of solution."[35] The broader the scope of politics, however, the more likely it is that it will include sets of antitheses that cut across and challenge the two-party line between political allies and enemies.* The long-term expansion of the reach of government, consequently, inherently threatens the kind of simplification that two-party politics presumes and requires. Our growing discontent with the two major parties, in other words, is only to be expected. In fact, given the diverging relationship between economics and culture, American opinion might suggest *four* parties rather than three; the division between Democrats and Republicans, for and against government intervention in the economy, is virtually bisected by the distinction between those

---

 * In this sense, militants for whom a particular stance on abortion is a political litmus test are only rejecting the *kind* of single-issue politics that divides Republicans and Democrats.

who support government intervention in moral and social life and those who oppose it. Republican libertarians sit as uneasily with cultural conservatives as Democratic liberals do with populist egalitarians.[36] Looking to 1996, Paul Tsongas has been promoting the possible candidacy of General Colin Powell, while Ross Perot seems more than willing to try again. And with disenchanted voters in the millions, such prospects have to be taken seriously.

But the winner-take-all form of our electoral system rules out third (and even more, fourth) parties, except in the very short term. With the partial exception of the Socialists early in this century, no American third party has managed to make a good showing in two successive elections. Voters hate to waste their votes if they see even a hair's-breadth of difference between leading candidates, and the major parties can be counted on to strengthen this logic by incorporating at least some of the appeals of any significant third party. Presuming that the electoral system remains as it is—and there is no serious movement to change it—a successful third party does not end the two-party system. It forces a redefinition of that system, and then passes, more or less gracefully, from the political scene. If a third party or candidacy does materialize in 1996, it can expect the same fate.

Still, American party politics *is* entering a new era. In 1992, almost everyone saw it: the age of the New Deal and the American century, virtual twins, are ending together—great, flawed times, and worth regretting, but sliding into memory. In American political history, the birth of a new party alignment, as Walter Dean Burnham observed, has ordinarily resulted from a "spasm" on the part of those middle American voters who are "normally content to be traditionalists or passive participants in electoral politics."[37] The election of 1994 showed some of the signs, but it involved too few voters and left too many Americans on the outside, unhappy with both alternatives and waiting for an engaging political story. It will challenge our crafts of state to ensure that any such narrative is worthy of American democracy.

Notes

1. "Republicans Like Both Previews and Reruns," *New York Times*, 12 December 1994, E1; Mickey Kaus, *The End of Equality* (New York: Basic Books, 1992).

2. Edward Luttwak, "America's Insecurity Blanket," *Washington Post National Weekly*, 5–11 December 1994, 23.

3. I quote from "Conversations with Gorbachev," broadcast on PBS's Channel 13, 1 January 1995.

4. Aristotle, *Politics*, 1294b.

5. *The Records of the Federal Convention of 1787*, ed. Max Farrand (New Haven and London: Yale University Press, 1911), 1:51, 135.

6. *The Federalist*, No. 63; *The Debates in the Several State Conventions, on the Adoption of the Federal Constitution*, ed. Jonathan Elliott (Philadelphia: Lippincott, 1907), 2:69, 222.

7. Sidney Verba, "The Voice of the People," *PS* 26 (1993): 678.

8. John Locke, *Second Treatise on Civil Government*, para. 96; see also Herbert McClosky, "The Fallacy of Absolute Majority Rule," *Journal of Politics* 11 (1949): 643.

9. George V. Higgins, *Victories* (New York: Henry Holt, 1990), 298.

10. Paul Kleppner, *Who Voted? The Dynamics of Electoral Turnout, 1870–1980* (New York: Praeger, 1982); John Petrocik, "Voter Turnout and Electoral Preference," in *Elections in America*, ed. Kay Lehman Schlozman (Boston: Allen and Unwin, 1987), 239–60.

11. Alexis de Tocqueville, *Democracy in America* (New York: Knopf, 1945), 2:105.

12. *Democracy in America*, 2:108–9, 116–17; Aristotle, *Politics*, 1252b, 1278b.

13. M.E. Olsen, "Social Participation and Voting Turnout," *American Sociological Review* 37 (1972): 317–33; G.D.H. Cole, *Essays in Social Theory* (London: Macmillan, 1950), 103–4.

14. Christopher Lasch, *The True and Only Heaven* (New York: Norton, 1991), 157, 165–66.

15. Mary Ann Glendon, *Rights Talk* (New York: Free Press, 1991); Benjamin Radcliff, "The Welfare State, Turnout and the Economy," *American Political Science Review* 86 (1992): 444–54.

16. Benjamin Ginsberg and Martin Shefter, *Politics by Other Means* (New York: Basic Books, 1990); James Q. Wilson, "The Newer Deal," *New Republic*, 2 July 1990, 34–36.

17. Walter Dean Burnham, "American Politics in the 1980s," *Dissent* 27 (1980): 155.

18. Gerald M. Pomper, "The Decline of the Party in American Elections," *Political Science Quarterly* 92 (1977): 21–41.

19. Stephen Salmore and Barbara Salmore, *Candidates, Parties and Campaigns* (Washington, D.C.: CQ Press, 1985); Thomas Byrne Edsall, *The New Politics of Inequality* (New York: Norton, 1984).

20. Steven E. Finkel, "Reexamining the 'Minimal Effects' Model in Recent Presidential Campaigns," *Journal of Politics* 55 (1993): 1–21.

21. Cole, *Essays in Social Theory,* 90–99; Tip O'Neill (with Gary Hymel), *All Politics is Local, and Other Rules of the Game* (New York: Random House, 1994).

22. Byron Shafer, "The New Cultural Politics," *PS* 18 (1985): 221–31.

23. L.E. Aylsworth, "The Passing of Alien Suffrage," *American Political Science Review* 25 (1931): 114–16.

24. Michael Barone, *Our Country: The Shaping of America from Roosevelt to Reagan* (New York: Free Press, 1990); William J. Crotty, "The Social Attributes of Party Organizational Activists in a Transitional Political System," *Western Political Quarterly* 20 (1967): 669–81.

25. Robert Dahl, "On Removing Certain Impediments to Democracy in the United States," *Political Science Quarterly* 92 (1977): 1–20.

26. David Carlin, "It's the Culture, Stupid," *Commonweal,* 23 September 1994, 9–10.

27. Sidney Verba and Gary Orren, *Equality in America* (Cambridge: Harvard University Press, 1985), 248–49.

28. John H. Schaar and Wilson C. McWilliams, "Uncle Sam Vanishes," *New University Thought* 1 (1961): 61–68.

29. H.L. Mencken, *Prejudices: A Selection,* ed. James T. Farrell (New York: Vintage, 1958), 47, 61.

30. David Carlin, "The Withering of the Working Class," *Commonweal,* 7 October 1994, 11–15; Christopher Lasch, *The Revolt of the Elites and the Betrayal of Democracy* (New York: Norton, 1995).

31. For example, Gunnar Myrdal, *An American Dilemma* (New York: Harper & Bros., 1944), 1:3–25.

32. *New York Times,* 10 January 1995, A1.

33. Walter Dean Burnham, "The End of American Party Politics," *Trans-Action* 7 (December 1969): 20; see also William G. Carleton, "The Passing of Bughouse Square," *Antioch Review* 20 (1960): 282–93.

34. Maurice Duverger, *Political Parties* (New York: John Wiley, 1963), 215–16.

35. Ibid., 215.

36. William S. Maddox and Stuart Λ. Lilic, *Beyond Liberal and Conservative* (Washington, D.C.: Cato Institute, 1984).

37. Burnham, "The End of American Party Politics," 20.

2

South Wind, Warning:
The Election of 1976

When you see the south wind blowing, you say, "There will be scorching heat," and it happens. You hypo-crites! You know how to interpret the appearance of earth and sky; why do you not know how to interpret the present time?

—Luke 12:55–56

For almost a hundred years," V.O. Key wrote in 1952, "ca-tastrophe has fixed the grand outlines of the partisan divi-sion among American voters."[1] Key had two disasters in mind: the Civil War, which created a solidly Democratic South; and the Great Depression, which established the Democrats as the party of working-class and low-income voters. After all the turbulence of the first quarter century, it seemed to be that tradi-tional coalition that elected Jimmy Carter in 1976.

On closer analysis, however, the election of 1976 shows that the old battle lines, though still very persistent, are chang-ing and yielding to more contemporary divisions. This, I argue, is especially evident in (1) the role of the South in the 1976 elec-tion, (2) Carter's relative weakness in northern industrial states, and (3) the increased salience of the "social issue" in electoral politics.

I also contend that all these aspects of the 1976 election are symptomatic of deeper challenges to American democracy. In the pattern of the 1976 campaign, in fact, there is more than a hint that a new period of soul-searching and trauma, if not "catastrophe" may await America. Certainly, the election of 1976 promises a changing and uncertain future for American party politics.

The Election

THE SOUTH

The Democratic South, the product of Key's first catastrophe, seemed to have passed into history before this year's election. Carter won more southern states than any other Democratic candidate since World War II. Disaffected by Democratic support for racial integration and disdain for "states' rights," traditional southern Democrats had experimented with third parties in 1948 and 1968 and, in increasing numbers, had turned to the Republican Party. Republicans were encouraged to hope that a presumably conservative South would form a reliable part of a "new Republican majority." Carter's near-sweep of the South was a terrible setback for this Republican "southern strategy." [2]

The election of 1976, however, did not represent a return to traditional southern Democracy. Carter carried a new South, decisively different from the "Solid South" that grew out of slavery, the Civil War, and Reconstruction.

In the first place, the traditional southern electorate was white, and Carter won only a minority of southern white voters. His victories depended on overwhelming black majorities and were possible only because the Voting Rights Acts of the 1960s had made it possible for previously disenfranchised blacks to register and vote.

Nevertheless, the sizable white minority that supported Carter was also crucial to his victory. It also points to major changes in the South. After all, blacks had voted in the South before, especially during Reconstruction. Then, however, southern whites voted with near unanimity to establish "white supremacy" and exclude blacks from political power. Blacks continued to vote down to the turn of the century, when fear of a coalition between radical populist whites and black voters helped to inspire the whole apparatus of laws designed to exclude black and poorer white voters from any effective suffrage. Many lower-class southern whites had, in effect, voted to disenfranchise themselves rather than endanger the edifice of "white supremacy."*

Architects of the "new Republican majority" always overestimated the conservatism of the white South. V.O. Key observed time and again that southern voters were, if anything, a bit more liberal on economic questions than voters elsewhere. As had been true in the 1890s, however, such liberal or radical economic attitudes tended to be checked, balanced, or outweighed by the desire to preserve a segregated and white-dominated society. Racism, not conservatism, was the key to the "southern strategy." Long before, Key had argued that only an "orgy of race hatred" could produce a Republican South.[3]

In the civil rights era, racial animosity certainly came to the surface. Violence was frequent, and something like an "orgy of race hatred" did develop. Even so, Lyndon Johnson lost only the Deep South states to Goldwater, and in 1968 many southerners preferred Wallace to Nixon. Nixon swept the South in 1972, but that was a national as well as a regional pattern. The violence and the hostility of the 1950s and 1960s was not enough, in other words, to create a Republican South despite southern bitterness toward the Democratic Party.

At the same time, more and more southern whites have accepted the end of segregation, at least as a fait accompli. Always, in the South, there had been courageous critics of the established order, and other southern whites had opposed segregation privately but kept silent from diplomacy or fear. Many

---

* On this period in southern politics, see C. Vann Woodward, *The Origins of the New South, 1877–1913* (Baton Rouge: Louisiana State University Press, 1951); and V.O. Key, *Southern Politics* (New York: Knopf, 1949), 533–54.

southern whites, too, had defended segregation because it was traditional, "the southern way of life," even though they doubted or rejected the racial theories used to justify the system. For this last group, segregation was often an embarrassment, and after a token resistance for "the honor of the flag," they were glad to see it go. Finally, even strong supporters of the old order found many reasons to be reconciled to its passing. Nightmarish visions of anarchy and rapine did not materialize. In fact, the South entered into a period of economic dynamism. When racial violence erupted in northern cities, shattering northern self-righteousness, the white South felt less uniquely stigmatized and even began a mild self-congratulation about how well—in comparison to the North—the South was managing the change in race relations. Increasingly, racism disappeared as an explicit concern of *public* policy, whatever people's private views and conduct.

This does not mean that southern whites, any more than their northern counterparts, have become racially enlightened. It does mean that southern whites do not reject—and are growing accustomed to—political cooperation with blacks. Excluding blacks from the political system is no longer a real option, even if whites desired it, and consequently appeals to "white solidarity" are relatively pointless. In the new political environment, "race issues" will continue to be important, but they will follow, rather than determine, the lines of party politics. In this respect, the South is simply becoming like the rest of the country.

Many southern white voters, of course, would not have voted Democratic if the candidate had not been a southerner. In the South, Carter benefited from the estrangement between the South and the country as a whole. The peculiar history of the South, beginning with slavery, has helped make southerners a "conscious minority."* And, in its turn, the rest of the country regards the South as culturally retarded. For a great many Americans, a southern accent is, prima facie, evidence of igno-

---

* The phrase is taken from Jesse Carpenter, *The South as a Conscious Minority* (New York: New York University Press, 1930).

rance, and southern institutions—like the Southern Baptist church—are considered quaint at best and probably backward. The gentlemanly "Rebs" of the old Westerns have yielded to slack-jawed, often malevolent "country boys," but stereotyped "southerners" still frequent the media. Lyndon Johnson wrote that he hesitated to run in 1964 because he doubted that a southern President could unite the country.

> I was not thinking just of the derisive articles about my style, my clothes, my manner, my accent and my family—although I admit I received enough of that kind of treatment in my first few months as President to last a lifetime. I was also thinking of . . . a disdain for the South that seems to be woven into the fabric of Northern experience. . . . Perhaps someday new understanding will cause this bias to disappear from our national life. I hope so, but it is with us still. *

Feeling scorned and resenting indignity, southerners have been inclined, like any minority, to defend their own.

Southern resentment and defensiveness are not limited to whites. To be sure, southern whites often consoled themselves for the humiliations they suffered at northern hands by inflicting worse injuries on blacks. But southern blacks *also* suffered from the prejudice against things southern, since their culture and institutions have been decisively shaped by the southern experience. In fact, since most black Americans have their cultural roots in the South, they are also affected. It seems likely, in fact, that once assured that Carter's belief in racial equality was genuine, many blacks voted for Carter *because* he was southern.

As the novelty of a southern President wears off, Carter and the Democrats may lose some of their new margin of strength in the region. Certainly Republican strategists hope this will be the case. But it seems equally likely that 1976 was a

---

* Lyndon B. Johnson, *The Vantage Point* (New York: Holt, Rinehart and Winston, 1971), 95. Johnson's feelings are especially notable because to many southerners he was more southwestern than southern.

"critical election," marking the conscious emergence of a post-segregation South, economically confident and eager for national recognition.* Jimmy Carter, a peanut farmer and a "born-again" Christian, was ideally suited to be the symbol of a South risen again. Possibly, as has been true at every juncture in recent American politics, the Democrats have come up on the right side of a critical election, identifying themselves with the feelings and aspirations of a people ready to make their claim for civic equality and dignity. The election of 1976, in other words, may have added a normal southern majority to the Democratic coalition.†

Familiarity, in any case, will add to Carter's strength in the North. All of his southern qualities emphasized, to northern voters, that Carter was an outsider and an unknown quantity. Urban Catholics and Jews suspected his evangelical Protestantism. The disastrous *Playboy* interview seems to have been intended to allay liberal fears that Carter might advocate censorship or other moralistic legislation. His mannerliness, too, seemed excessive to voters who wanted him to voice their indignation. This sort of anxiety and suspicion will almost certainly dissipate as the country becomes accustomed to Carter and his style.‡ But the fact that it existed in 1976 illumined another dimension of contemporary American politics.

---

* On the concept of "critical elections," see Walter Dean Burnham, *Critical Elections and the Mainsprings of American Politics* (New York: Norton, 1970).

† *Obviously, this guess, though guarded, was dead wrong, even though Carter did relatively well in the South in 1980. In retrospect, I should have recognized that conservative Protestantism (and the broader sense of cultural marginality) was becoming increasingly salient at the expense of economic distinctions, foreshadowing today's "culture wars" and a less ambiguously conservative tone to southern politics.*—Author note, 1995.

‡ *Familiarity did lessen anxiety about Carter, but not the feeling that he was distinctly odd, perhaps especially in his moralism. And any gains he made with the voters were more than balanced by the growing belief in his ineptitude.*—Author note, 1995.

THE ELECTION AND THE ECONOMY

No principle of recent political analysis has been more firmly enshrined than the belief that high unemployment rates portend a Democratic landslide. Since the Great Depression, the Democrats have been regarded as the party of labor and associated with government intervention to reduce unemployment. Time and again, voters have declared that they trust the Democrats to run the economy more than they trust Republicans. In economic affairs, Americans tend to see the GOP as inept and hostile, the party of business ranged against the interests of "the little guy." Republicans have virtually conceded the point, seeking to counter this Democratic advantage by arguing—as both President Ford and Senator Dole did in 1976—that Democrats produced full employment in the past only by leading the country into war. It is not a very sound argument, although it is sometimes persuasive, but the attempt to categorize the Democrats as the "war party" is some indication of Republican despair whenever the election turns on economic issues alone.

By that standard, 1976 should have been a Democratic triumph in all the industrial states. Unemployment rates were higher than they had been since the depression and they had been high during the whole Nixon-Ford term. The administration trumpeted a "recovery" that barely dented those alarming figures. Already able to run against Nixon and Watergate, the Democrats were also able to run against Hoover and the depression.

In the congressional election, something like a Democratic landslide did develop. Democrats held the gains they had made in the "Watergate election" of 1974, retaining many seats once regarded as safely Republican. In the presidential election, however, Gerald Ford did very well in states where unemployment might have been expected to hurt him badly. Even where Carter won, his margins were closer than expected, and Ford carried two states in the deeply depressed industrial Northeast (New Jersey and Connecticut), dominated the industrial Midwest, and swept the Far West. A more familiar, less culturally alien Democrat—Edward Kennedy, for example—might have won a number of states where critical blocs of voters, alarmed by Carter's strangeness, voted for "the devil we know." Certainly the Ford campaign made excellent use of the presidency to emphasize the tried-and-true safety of their candidate. Nevertheless, the fact that normally Democratic voters would defect to Ford despite the ramshackle condition of the economy says a good deal about the decline of the feelings and loyalties that grew out of the Great Depression.

Voters who preferred Ford were likely to worry about inflation and taxes more than they feared unemployment. And politically, it is the *fear* of unemployment that matters; even in the worst periods, only a fraction of the labor force is actually unemployed.

Traditionally, it took very few layoffs to make almost all workers uneasy and anxious about their jobs. Before the New Deal and the rise of organized labor, the decision to hire and fire was an employer's prerogative. Senior and highly paid workers, who had the most to lose, had reason to fear that they would "get the sack" in difficult times. Skill was sometimes a source of security, but as Marx had observed, industrial technology tended to displace skilled workers in favor of unskilled, less expensive labor. Unemployment was close to an ultimate calamity because few workers had any resources other than their jobs, and almost no one felt safe once layoffs began.

Now, many workers feel reasonably secure despite high rates of unemployment. A large number of workers feel that their jobs are protected by seniority rights, job tenure, or other provisions of agreements between employers and employees. Both collective bargaining and bureaucracy tend to protect senior employees against arbitrary firings and make it much easier, if layoffs are necessary, for employers to discharge new employees—who are disproportionately young, poor, and nonwhite. The "two-tiered economy" exists inside the bureau or the factory.

Unemployment is still a real danger, of course, even for relatively protected workers. Such workers are, however, insulated against short-term economic fluctuations. Unemployment becomes a relatively distant worry, not to be compared with immediate problems like paying the bills out of a paycheck depleted by taxes and shrunk by inflation. Workers who feel shielded against unemployment are likely to demand that unions win cost-of-living increases even if, in hard times, this means unemployment among the newly hired. And similarly, workers who are nearing retirement worry less about teenage unemployment than they do about the impact of inflation on their pension funds.

These relatively privileged workers are part of the "contract society," a growing mass of Americans—ranging from secure organized labor to upper-middle-class professionals—whose position depends on statutes and contracts as much as skill, and who are exempted from the logic of the market. Their advantages derive from the organized power of interest groups and collective agents, and they rely on public authority to support or actively promote their private interests (for example, through licensing laws that allow professionals to control the supply of labor). Most members of the contract society feel secure barring a major social upheaval, and it is no surprise if they shy away from uncertainty and distrust change.

None of this is new. Social theorists have been describing this evolving pattern for a good many years.[4] Nearly a quarter-century ago, Samuel Lubell suggested that this sort of development might lead erstwhile Democrats into the Republican Party.[5] Lubell erred in stressing interest too much and memory too little. Workers who had entered the work force in or before the 1930s' depression, and those who grew up during the depression years, remembered the old economy with its omnipresent threat of unemployment—and the memory colored their reaction to changes in the unemployment rate. Now, the old economy seems very distant if people remember it at all. Members of the contract society are increasingly inclined toward fiscal conservatism. They do not want to pay high taxes; they distrust "big spenders"; they are suspicious of bureaucracy. After a few missteps, Carter responded to this current of opinion, emphasizing his own concern for fiscal restraint and a balanced budget. In general, members of the contract society must be persuaded to support change. They own shares in the ship and are not eager to rock the boat.

This turn of mind provides Republicans with a great opportunity to win converts from the Democratic majority, but it is an opportunity that will probably go unused. Although the members of the contract society have conservative tendencies, they want to conserve the America created by the New Deal. Few Americans, Archie Bunker aside, believe that we could "use a man like Herbert Hoover again." The Republican insistence on speaking the language of economic individualism, assailing "big labor" and defending "the private sector," does not attract the "children of the New Deal" whose position presumes an active, protective government and who see organized labor as at least a vital part of American society.[6]

During the campaign, President Ford—like Nixon in 1972 —found it necessary to play down his party and to praise Democratic leaders like Harry Truman. But it is doubtful that admiration for Truman—now something of a vogue—would lead many Republican leaders to advocate the Fair Deal in Republican primaries. The Republican right, the survival of another era in American politics, makes it all but impossible for the Republicans to change in the direction of the electorate. Conservative southerners were once a problem for the Democrats, but after Roosevelt they never had a decisive voice or veto in party councils. The Republican right, by contrast, has grown stronger with time, as President Ford learned in 1976. On the basis of the past record, Republicans will miss their chance to win the economic confidence of the American center, and Democrats will continue to enjoy the allegiance of workers in the contract society as well as those outside it who are most vulnerable to unemployment.[7]

THE SOCIAL ISSUE

In recent years, the "social issue" has been an important Republican asset.[1] In 1968, concern about crime and civil disorder led many voters to desert the Democrats. Similarly, in 1972, McGovern's positions on abortion, marijuana, and an amnesty for deserters and draft evaders were generally considered to have hurt him among traditional Democrats.

Carter's relative social conservatism lessened the impact of such issues in 1976. Some voters probably defected to Ford because Carter did not support an antiabortion amendment to the Constitution. Others may have been offended that Carter proposed to pardon draft evaders, although the Appalachian region—militantly hostile to amnesty in 1972—was a Carter stronghold. Since Carter insisted that a pardon, unlike an amnesty, presumes the wrongness of the acts being forgiven, he disarmed many potential critics. Thus, candidate choice in this year was not closely related to alternative positions on the general "social issue."

But the 1976 election was almost unique in the intrusive attention devoted to the private lives and personal beliefs of the candidates. Inevitably, after the Watergate scandal, candidates were expected to be persons of unquestioned probity. This year, however, candidates were subjected to a scrutiny that went far beyond a concern for personal integrity. Carter felt compelled to discuss his code of sexual behavior. Mrs. Ford discussed premarital sex and marijuana, as did Mrs. Carter, and the candidates' children commented, with apparent frankness, on their parents' ideas. Neither candidate, probably, gained many converts because of these performances, although the *Playboy* interview undoubtedly hurt Carter. It is more notable that such questions should be asked and answered. Until quite recently, it would have been assumed that presidential candidates held traditional beliefs about private morality and, in the unlikely event that they held differing views, would not offend the electorate by saying so. In any case, such matters were *private*, not appropriate subjects for public prying and discussion, and a reporter who raised them openly would have been seen as intolerably impertinent.

Obviously, in 1976 candidates and voters alike considered that "private" moral beliefs *had* become public issues. Part of this, undoubtedly, was due to Watergate. Raised in the belief that the checks and balances of the Constitution made it a self-regulating mechanism that radically reduced our dependence on public virtue and enlightened statesmen, Americans were shaken by the crisis. The Constitution weathered the storm, but a less inept usurper than Mr. Nixon might have survived, and the whole affair emphasized how much contemporary America *does* depend on the president's character and virtue.

Moreover, for some years, "private" issues have been forcing their way into public places. Racial discrimination in private clubs—not to mention private corporations and trade unions—has been a matter of public concern for some time. The women's movement has made sex roles into political questions. Lifestyle issues such as hair length and sexual preference have troubled great public institutions like the army.[9] Republicans have tended to gain most from the introduction of these issues. Divided between voters who adhere to traditional beliefs and advocates of new social patterns and moral standards, Democrats have learned to tread warily. Comments hostile to homosexuals are thought to have damaged Senator Henry Jackson's campaign in the 1976 New York primary, but any other statement would have weakened the senator's hold on his traditional working-class supporters. Senator McGovern was helped in the primaries in 1972 by the very "social" positions that helped derail his campaign in the general election. But although Democrats have suffered most, Republicans have not gone unscathed. It certainly did Republicans no good, for example, when President Nixon—so sententious in public—was revealed to be extremely foul-mouthed in private. Voters were bound to suspect, at least, that Republican moral professions were only hypocrisies.

All politicians and parties have been buffeted by the intrusion of traditionally private issues into public realms. In fact, the "social issue" reflects a changing idea of the very *meaning* of politics and political life in America.[10]

The Meanings

THE ELECTION AND THE AMERICAN TRADITION

Political theorists point out that our definition of politics shapes our fundamental ideas about political things. Traditionally, Americans have regarded the meaning of politics as self-evident, needing no explanation. As in so many things, Americans accepted the political ideas that we had received from the Framers. In recent years, however, American complacency has been shaken; the election of 1976 may be a sign that it has been shattered, and the American political tradition itself has become an issue.

The "science of politics" on which the Framers based the Constitution presumed that politics should not concern itself with the fundamentals of morality. The Framers believed that human beings were naturally free, self-preserving, and self-seeking and that they created government for limited purposes, ceding some "natural rights" and retaining others. First, government existed to protect citizens against each other and against outsiders; second, it was intended to help them in their quest for power and for mastery over nature. Government was needed to restrain vice and advance interests. It was not the job of government to shape human character and moral personality. That task was reserved for "society," the private world of families, churches, and communities. In Thomas Paine's famous definition, "Society is produced by our wants and government by our wickedness; the former promotes our happiness *positively* by uniting our affections, the latter *negatively* by restraining our vices." [11]

But the Framers worried, given their concern to protect individual freedom, that the emotional hold of local communities would be too strong, restricting liberty and retarding progress. And in part, the Framers simply took the existence of strong families, churches, and communities for granted. In any case, they gave most of their attention to "freeing" the individual from excessive social control, even though this involved undermining the position and prerogatives of society.

But even the Framers did not doubt that government depended on and could support social institutions. Governments had the right to safeguard the "health, morals and safety" of their citizens. Within their jurisdictions, governments could define and protect marriage, just as they could assign authority over children and regulate their education. They could define life and the right to take it. And through taxation and the regulation of commerce, they could shape the world of work, property, and exchange. The line between state and society was far from absolute, and the character of government depended on the "wisdom and firmness" of the people.

Some leaders of the early Republic went a good deal beyond the Framers in this respect. "Statesmen," John Adams wrote, "may plan and speculate for Liberty, but it is Religion and Morality alone which can establish the Principles upon which Freedom can securely stand. . . . The only foundation of a free Constitution is pure Virtue."[12] Moreover, despite considerable diversity, the "private order" of families, churches, and communities spoke in terms of a common teaching. Human beings, in that traditional creed, were naturally dependent, social, and political animals. They needed the common life to develop emotional security, moral faculties, and personal identity. Individualism and self-seeking ran contrary to human nature rightly understood; self-mastery and self-knowledge were essential elements of true freedom, and what was "naturally right" mattered more than "natural rights." It was that substantive tradition that Alexis de Tocqueville had in mind when he argued that free institutions in America were maintained more by American customs than by American laws.[13]

In the past, Americans found their emotional security and learned their substantive beliefs in the private order. There they found the social and moral security that made it possible to accept the uncertainties of a public universe characterized by individualism, conflict, and change. Individual freedom was the tip of the iceberg; the real foundation was provided by the traditional creeds that set limits to freedom and that defined the uses to which freedom should be put. "Our constitution," Adams declared, "was made only for a moral and religious people. It is wholly inadequate to the government of any other."[14]

CONTEMPORARY CHALLENGES

In 1976, Americans were painfully aware that the traditional teachings were fading and that the social and moral "givens" of the past were under attack where they survived at all. Rather consistently, the private order has been weakened and undermined in American history; now it approaches collapse. A national economy made local communities and governments less important, and almost impotent, in dealing with the vital economic sphere of life. Unable to rely on locality, Americans have been encouraged by increasing mobility—especially in the age of the automobile—to move in response to economic currents, breaking their ties with friends and family. In the pain of leaving and being left, we learn to minimize our commitments to new friends and homes.

Too, organizations that are large enough to be effective in advancing our interests tend to be so large that we are dwarfed, and we withdraw into private spheres where we have the sense that we matter. The media, however, pursue us into our most intimate retreats, entering the home and probing for the deepest corners of the mind. Local beliefs and cultures lose autonomy and control. More and more, we feel isolated in a world of mass and change that we can neither understand nor control, and in which we are hard pressed to maintain any psychological or moral autonomy. A growing number of Americans simply drift in the social current, relating to others only through style and image, making few deep commitments, finding little intimacy and less meaning.

Americans doubt the stability and continuity of ultimate retreats like the family. Changing sex roles threaten traditional family patterns. Established moral codes are publicly defied and ridiculed. Inevitably, many Americans are driven to ask whether they can "count on" enough to make it worthwhile to sacrifice for the future. Perfect security, of course, is impossible: blacksmiths once thought they had a stable trade. But if citizens are to make any commitments at all, they need the sense that some things are relatively predictable, stable, and continuing. Even if we think of law and morals as no more than "rules of the game," it ought to be obvious that if the rules change in the middle of the game, people will wonder if it makes sense to "play fair." We should not be surprised if more and more Americans are inclined to "take care of number one." Early in the nineteenth century, Alexis de Tocqueville commented that democratic individualism makes

> every man forget his ancestors ... hides his descendents, and separates his contemporaries from him; it throws him back for ever upon himself alone, and threatens in the end to confine him entirely within the solitude of his own heart.[15]

These tendencies alarm Americans even as they reflect and adjust to them. It has become a popular truth in our time that when freedom is reduced to "just another word for nothing left to lose," people will wish to abandon or escape from freedom. Public and political freedom depends on private and personal security, which makes it necessary to attempt to rebuild the links between citizens and generations, strengthening social ties, local communities and the "art of association" that Tocqueville regarded as vital to the future of democracy. Concern about the social issue is based on a recognition, however inarticulate and incomplete, of the need to restore the civic bond.

This is no longer a private problem. As recent politics suggests, issues such as sex roles, the structure and duties of the family, and the limits and powers of local communities have become public questions in which action by public authority is critical. Dominated by the liberal belief in the separation of state and society, government has paid little attention to rebuilding or reconstructing the private order. Instead, it has allowed and even encouraged social fragmentation.[16] The record of local communities in the past has certainly been bad enough to merit watchfulness—the Old South is example enough—and bureaucratic corporations are hardly "voluntary organizations" in the old image of society. But the sins of the old private order and the defects of contemporary social life do not argue for a world *without* moral foundations or social security; they strengthen the case for reconstruction.

POLITICAL PARTIES AND THE FUTURE

Historically, concern for social order has been associated with conservatives. Nevertheless, the need to reconstruct the private order seems a Democratic opportunity to turn the "social issue" into a Democratic asset. In the first place, established American conservatism rejects government intervention except to punish malefactors and seems to presume a healthy society, able to care for itself if left alone. American conservatism is, in fact, an ossified form of philosophic liberalism, highly individualistic and strongly committed to technological progress and social change. Conservatives bemoan social decay, but they also encourage the forces that promote it.* In principle at least, Democrats seem better suited to the use of public power to strengthen the civic bond, encouraging new forms of private order while protecting those parts of the old private order that remain viable. Carter's expressed concern for the family and for ethnic culture could easily coexist with interest in new analogues of the extended family and with ideas of community control.

---

*   *In the Gingrich era, given the Speaker's fondness for technology's revolutions, this observation takes on special force.*—Author note, 1995.

There are no grounds for believing that this will happen, however. Like the Americans who elected him, Jimmy Carter is divided between his traditional, religious morality and his commitment to scientific management and to the liberal creed that shaped our formal institutions. Many Democrats, moreover, wedded to individualistic ideas of personal liberty, see nothing alarming in the decay of the old order and often applaud its demise. There are fewer reasons to believe that Carter and the Democrats will *rise* to the challenge of an "age of reconstruction" than there are reasons to believe that Republicans will *fail* it.[17] We may, in fact, stand at the beginning of a period of one-party rule not unlike the years during which the Federalist Party languished and died and the dominant Jeffersonians stagnated.*

In any case, all political parties have an interest in addressing the social issue and in seeking to rebuild the foundations of civic community. The historic bases of party identification are weakening, and the new ties are fragile. Citizens in "limited liability communities" do not make strong partisans.[18] They restrict their trust in parties and leaders as they limit their commitments to their fellow citizens. Strong democratic parties require a strong private order, and democratic government requires strong political parties to make government responsive to citizens and to make citizens devoted to law and the common good.

In fact, however, American political parties have grown weaker. The direct primary, designed to weaken party organization, has now become nearly universal.[19] The Campaign Reform Act gives public money to individual candidates, treating politi-

---

* *This prediction was off the mark, but I was in good company: Ronald Reagan, for one, thought the Republicans so endangered that he proposed changing the party's name* (Richard Berke, "Epic Political Realignments Often Aren't," *New York Times*, 1 January 1995, E3). *And in a sense I was right. Stagnant or in decline, the Democrats remained the dominant party even though they lost the presidency three times running, controlling the Senate for twelve of the next eighteen years, and the House until 1995.*—Author note, 1995.

cal relationships as bonds between leaders and followers, not as ties between citizens. Moreover, while campaign legislation limits the total amount that a candidate may spend, it permits this money to be spent as the candidate decides. In 1976, both candidates understandably opted to use almost all their limited funds on the mass media, radically reducing efforts to involve citizens and to encourage local organization and participation. This decreased the extent to which the election was a civic and public event. This aspect of the campaign law has been widely criticized, and it seems likely to be corrected. One must hope it will be. As it stands, federal law seems to encourage a politics based almost solely on leaders who relate to followers through the mass media. That is closer to the model of totalitarian parties than it is to traditional democratic ideals.

In 1976, Carter tapped feelings of alienation from the federal government, seen by more and more citizens as a distant, impersonal bureaucracy. Carter's arguments in favor of a reorganized and simplified government that citizens can understand are part of the Jeffersonian tradition. But Jefferson also recognized that citizens need a government that is *responsive*. Today, citizens constantly depend on government, and they have even greater needs for a sense of connection to it and for ways of being heard. Political parties in which citizens are more than spectators are essential to a proper relation between citizen and government.

In fact, political parties are especially vital given our new political anxieties. In 1976, Americans were worried about the most basic aspects of political identity; they were concerned with the social and moral foundations of community, and they felt the need for ties with *each other* as much as or more than they felt the need of ties to Washington. Political parties can themselves—through local organizations and citizen participation—be part of a new network of ties among citizens.

The old limits on government, the mechanical "balances" and statutes designed to keep government out of our lives, are now evidently inadequate. We need government in our lives to strengthen, and in some cases to create, "society." But government that enters our lives so pervasively can easily be despotic without new kinds of restraint. Limited government in 1976 depends less on self-regulated mechanisms and more on citizen-regulated politics. Political parties have done more than express the needs and feelings of citizens. They have educated them in the norms and values of democratic politics. With some justice, George Washington Plunkitt asserted that "the parties built this great country."[20] And the ideal of civic education through revitalized parties is certainly attractive, only eight years from 1984.

Notes

1. V.O. Key, Jr., "The Future of the Democratic Party," *Virginia Quarterly* 28 (1952): 161.

2. Kevin Phillips, *The Emerging Republican Majority* (New York: Arlington, 1969).

3. Key, "Future of the Democratic Party," 173; see also Key's *Public Opinion and American Democracy* (New York: Knopf, 1961).

4. For example, see J.A.C. Grant, "The Gild Returns to America," *Journal of Politics* 4 (1942): 303–36, 458–77; John Kenneth Galbraith, *American Capitalism: The Concept of Countervailing Power* (Boston: Houghton Mifflin, 1952); Grant McConnell, *Private Power and American Democracy* (New York: Knopf, 1966); and Theodore Lowi, *The End of Liberalism* (New York: Norton, 1969).

5. Samuel Lubell, *The Future of American Politics* (New York: Harper, 1952); see also Lubell's *The Revolt of the Moderates* (New York: Harper, 1956); and *The Hidden Crisis in American Politics* (New York: Norton, 1970).

6. Richard Centers, "Children of the New Deal: Social Stratification and Adolescent Attitudes," *International Journal of Opinion and Attitude Research* 4 (1950): 315–35.

7. Herbert McClosky et al., "Issue Conflict and Consensus among Party Leaders and Followers," *American Political Science Review* 54 (1960): 406–27, describes the continuing Republican problem.

8. For the concept of the "social issue," see Richard Scammon and Ben Wattenberg, *The Real Majority* (New York: Coward McCann, 1970).

9. William L. Hauser, *America's Army in Crisis* (Baltimore: Johns Hopkins University Press, 1973).

10. Nancy R. McWilliams, "Contemporary Feminism, Consciousness-Raising and Changing Views of the Political," in *Women in Politics,* ed. Jane Jaquette (New York: John Wiley, 1974), 157–70.

11. Thomas Paine, *Common Sense and Other Political Writings* (New York: Liberal Arts Press, 1953), 4.

12. L.H. Butterfield, ed., *Adams Family Correspondence* (New York: Atheneum, 1965), 2:20–21.

13. Alexis de Tocqueville, *Democracy in America* (New York: Vintage, 1957), vol. 1, chap. 17.

14. Cited in John Howe, *The Changing Political Thought of John Adams* (Princeton, N.J.: Princeton University Press, 1966), 185.

15. Tocqueville, *Democracy in America,* vol. 2, bk. 2, chap. 3.

16. Walter Berns, *The First Amendment and the Future of American Democracy* (New York: Basic Books, 1967).

17. The phrase "age of reconstruction" is taken from Karl Mannheim, *Man and Society in an Age of Reconstruction* (New York: Harcourt, Brace, 1951).

18. For the concept of "limited liability community," see Scott Greer, "Individual Participation in Mass Society," in *Approaches to the Study of Politics,* ed. Roland Young (Evanston, Ill.: Northwestern University Press, 1958), 329 42.

19. For an extended critique of the primary system, see my essay "Down with the Primaries," *Commonweal* 103 (2 July 1976): 427–29.

20. William Riordan, *Plunkitt of Tammany Hall* (New York: Dutton, 1963).

3

Presidential Leadership and Changing Parties: The Election of 1980

Stand fast in your enchantments and your many sorceries, with which you have labored from your youth; perhaps you may be able to succeed, perhaps you may inspire terror.

—Isaiah 47:12

I t didn't mean much. The election of 1980 did not try our souls; it tried our patience. Matthew Josephson's description of the election of 1880 applied a century later: "the indifference of the public seems as marked as the excitement of the professionals seems feigned."*

Reagan had a zealous following and there were some Carter loyalists, but most voters saw little to recommend either. Carter was a humorless bungler and Reagan was an amiable

---

* Matthew Josephson, *The Politicos* (New York: Harcourt, Brace, 1938), 287. There are other suggestive similarities between the elections of 1980 and 1880. In 1880, the minority Democrats nominated their closest equivalent of a movie star, a handsome Union general, Winfield Scott Hancock, a hero of Gettysburg famed for his copious and wide-ranging profanity. General Hancock's economics were also as weirdly imaginative as Ronald Reagan's: he once described the tariff as a "local question." E.E. Robinson, *The Evolution of Political Parties* (New York: Harcourt, Brace, 1924), 198–99.

simpleton, "the Ted Baxter of American politics."* Even the enthusiasm for John Anderson was negative, deriving from distaste for the major-party nominees. A good many voters marked
their ballots in a mood of revulsion, and masses of citizens
stayed home. The majority of voters finally decided, probably
on the basis of the presidential debate, that Reagan was not so
kooky as to keep them from gratifying their desire to be rid of
Carter. Reagan will have four years to try his hand, but Americans stopped believing in progress in 1980, and few of them feel
any confidence in the new experiment. That is the central meaning of the election of 1980.†

The election does have other things to tell us. In the first
place, the election of 1980 made it clear that the primary-dominated system of nomination is an unqualified disaster. Second,
among Democrats, the old Roosevelt coalition is yielding to
something we can call the Kennedy coalition. Third, conservative Republicanism is experiencing its own, analogous change,
and conservatism may find victory more painful than defeat.
The election may, of course, prove to have far more profound
and far-reaching consequences for American politics, but no
such portents are visible. We will have to wait and see.

The Failure of the Primaries

In 1980, there were more primaries than ever and a record number of voters participated in choosing the candidates. Yet, in a

---

* This wonderful description of Reagan was coined by Mike
Royko, "Maybe It's Better to Know Nothing," *Star-Ledger*, 8 November
1980.

† *I understand the extent to which Reagan's election reflected a
distrust of government. Still, the most important "meaning" of 1980
grew out of the Reagan presidency, especially given Reagan's gift of
understanding and working an audience, combined with a disposition to
back away from anything too painful or militant in the conservative
agenda, a caution apparently encouraged by Mrs. Reagan. And finally,
Reagan, unlike Carter, enjoyed a striking run of good luck at least until
the Iran-*contra *affair*—Author note, 1995.

seeming paradox, the result was radically unpopular. By any standard, the primaries failed as a method of choosing presidential candidates.

Primaries have been around since the Progressive era; but until the last decade, nominations resulted from a mixed system in which most delegates were chosen by state conventions and candidates tried to show popular appeal in a few, carefully selected contests. In 1948, for example, Thomas E. Dewey was able to offset Harold Stassen's string of primary victories by defeating him in Oregon after a debate, heard nationwide, in which Dewey opposed and Stassen advocated outlawing the Communist party.[1] Similarly, when John F. Kennedy defeated Hubert H. Humphrey in West Virginia in 1960, he dispelled the fear that his Catholicism would be a fatal liability in Protestant areas, or at least lessened such anxieties enough to let him win the nomination. But primaries, if often decisive, were only one part of the nominating process. Adlai Stevenson was drafted at the 1952 Democratic convention, and as late as 1968, Hubert Humphrey was nominated without seriously contesting, let alone winning, any primaries. Humphrey's victory, however, was *finis:* the disastrous Chicago convention of 1968 set in motion the torrent of reform. Since 1968, the number of primaries has roughly doubled, and about three-fourths of the delegates are now chosen in primary elections.

The record of the new, primary-dominated system is not impressive. Since the election of 1968, not one first-rate person has been nominated for president. It could easily be argued that Richard Nixon was the most able of the major-party nominees. Of course, the old system sometimes selected mediocrities. The choice between Harding and Cox in 1920 was at least as limited as our options in 1980. Yet in the eighteen presidential elections between 1900 and 1968, only ten nominations went to candidates who are even arguably second-rate.* Twenty-six major-party nominations went to evidently first-rate people. For the

---

* I have tried to make my list inclusive: I count Coolidge, Cox, Davis, Goldwater, Harding, Landon, McKinley, Nixon, and Parker, al-

"smoke-filled room," mediocrity was the *exception;* for the primary-dominated system, it has been the *rule.*

The primaries fail because they are based on the assumption that voting in elections is the essence of democracy. At most, however, voting is the *final* act of the democratic process, deciding between alternatives that have been defined by some sort of deliberation.

Voting forces a decision. Our choices are limited, *and the more limited they are,* the more clearly we know the consequences of our choice. If there are two candidates, by voting for one I am voting against the other. But if there are three serious candidates (as it briefly seemed there might be in 1980), if I vote for Anderson, it is not at all clear that I am voting against Reagan and Carter. If I hate Carter and would prefer Reagan, then I am helping Carter by voting for Anderson. Added alternatives make voting complicated and confusing.

This is especially true since my vote is *irrevocable.* I cannot take it back once I see which way the wind is blowing or after I have second thoughts. If I could change my vote, third candidates would not be so confusing; I could vote for a third-party candidate and wait to see if he or she could make a race of it. If not, I could fall back on one of the front-runners. As it is, however, voting encourages us to narrow our alternatives, concentrating on the two leading candidates so that the meaning of our vote is clear: for *A,* against *B.* Even with a more or less proportional distribution of delegates, so that one does not "throw away" a vote for a third candidate, this narrowing tendency is evident in the primaries. In the last stages of this year's campaign, only two candidates remained in each party. An election aims at a clear and irrevocable decision and encourages voters to limit their alternatives.

Deliberation, by contrast, attempts to define the terms of choice rather than to decide between them. In deliberating, we

---

though Professor Harry Jaffa is engaged in the attempt to rehabilitate Coolidge, and others on this list—like Landon and Goldwater—are men of parts by our contemporary standards.

value all the complications and flexibilities that elections aim to rule out. We want to avoid limiting our choices prematurely. We want to consider all possible alternatives all the candidates who might run, for example, not merely those who have announced so far. Similarly, deliberation encourages the exchange of views; it values second thoughts, changed minds, and modified opinions. It is not enough to express our opinions; we need a chance to respond to other opinions. This response is more than "compromise"; it involves the chance for considered judgment, rendered after weighing (and counting) the opinions of others. We want the best chance to refine our thinking before decision; hence, *Robert's Rules of Order* allows a minority to keep debate open. And even after we decide, *Robert's Rules* allows us, with appropriate constraints, the chance to reconsider. Finally, deliberation aims at agreement or broad consensus, hoping that discussion will obviate the need for decision. Deliberation, then, puts off decisions, multiplies alternatives, permits considered judgment, and strives for consensus.

In nominating a candidate for president, only one vote is *necessary,* the final ballot of the party's convention. All the rest of the process, although it involves decisions to select delegates in the several states, is or ought to be deliberative. Evidently, the party's most authoritative decision only establishes an alternative for the voters in the general election. The nomination is the last step in a process of deliberation and the first step of a contest leading to an electoral decision.

The primary-dominated system, by contrast, all but displaces deliberation. In the first place, primary elections limit us because they demand *early* decisions by candidates. It is quite possible that a majority of Democrats in 1980 would have preferred some candidate other than President Carter or Senator Kennedy. "The voters don't want us," a Carter loyalist told me on the eve of the Florida primary, "but they don't want *them* even more." A great many Republican voters would have preferred President Ford to Ronald Reagan, including a great many who preferred Reagan to George Bush. Ford himself was eager to prevent Reagan's nomination, and when it became likely, Ford offered to run himself. Ford, however, had delayed too long; he would not have been able to enter enough primaries to change the result. Possibly Ford was genuinely unwilling to run unless a Reagan nomination threatened; possibly he secretly hoped, all along, that the party would turn to him. In either case, Ford's experience in 1980 (and Senator Humphrey's in 1976) indicates that our primaries demand that candidates decide early. They cannot respond to events or change their minds.

The primaries thus deprive us of the most powerful argument for persuading excellent people to seek office: the fear that they will otherwise be ruled by second-raters or worse.[2] By the time that such a threat has become credible, it is likely to be too advanced to be evitable.

Similarly, early support matters much more than considered support. Since voters tend to choose between candidates they feel have a "real chance" of winning, a tide runs in favor of candidates who establish themselves as front-runners. Voters in early primaries have a disproportionate influence on events. Several big states (with about 20 percent of the convention delegates) voted on "Super Tuesday," 3 June, after the nominations were effectively decided. It would take away this advantage, of course, if we all voted on the same day, but then *only* early support would matter because voters would have no chance to react to or learn from the elections in other states.

In becoming a front-runner, established celebrities have an edge. Carter won as a dark horse in 1976, but he ran against a field of unknowns. It also helps to have an enthusiastic, ideological following. Even if you don't win, your zealots may keep you among the leaders. And you will have a good chance to win; primary voters are not representative of the party as a whole, and highly committed voters are likely to have disproportionate influence.[3] In the early primaries, moreover, against a fragmented opposition, an ideological following may enable a candidate to win with less than a majority, as Ronald Reagan often did in 1980. Senator George McGovern in 1972 won a similar victory by establishing himself as the candidate of the Democratic Left. Senator Edmund Muskie, an acceptable second choice for almost all factions, was driven from the race. The primaries have small place for second choices, even though, like second thoughts, such selections are more likely to reflect a concern for the good of the whole.

The media, of course, play an enormous role in selecting front-runners. In the first place, media predictions tell voters where their "real choice" lies. More important, the media can create an important candidacy by coverage alone, as they certainly did with Congressman Anderson in 1980. The problem does not lie with the supposed ideological biases of the media; the worst distortions result from the desire to make political news exciting. Anderson was noteworthy in early Republican gatherings because he said strikingly different things. In 1972, by contrast, the press severely damaged Senator Muskie by focusing on his crying during a speech in Manchester, New Hampshire. Moreover, while it is important to win primaries, a victor must do "as well as expected" by the media, and a losing candidate who fares better than the polls predict may establish himself as a serious contender. A "good" loss inspires supporters in subsequent states, just as a "bad" victory dispirits them. Muskie lost ground by winning New Hampshire in 1972, and Senator Henry Jackson's candidacy could not survive his victory in New York in 1976. As James Ceaser writes, "the media love the story, which is to say that they tend to look for, and overplay, new and unexpected developments. Thus they turn politics into drama, rather than reporting on the drama of politics."[4] At their best, the media encourage us to react to more or less accurate images, which we have no means of checking.

In short, the primaries give special weight to initial support for candidates who enter early, they advantage ideological followings, and they emphasize media images. They discourage considered judgment and place no particular value on party coalitions. They violate all the requirements of deliberation in precisely that aspect of our electoral process—the choosing of nominees—where deliberateness is most needed.

The older system of precinct and ward caucuses, leading to county and state conventions, was, even at its worst, based on discussion and personal knowledge of the candidates. The deliberation that occurred was often crass, ungrammatical, and parochial, but it *was* deliberation for all that. It was based on local, face-to-face groups where real discussion and participation was possible and where people could select representatives who reflected the gamut of their views. The fault of the old system was simple: it shut people out. Party organizations were too often closed and unresponsive, denying citizens (and partisans) a role in an essential democratic process. But this shortcoming did not reflect on the convention system; it militated against excluding people *from* that system.

The logical reform would have been a more or less open caucus, similar to the present system in Iowa. Instead, the reform tradition insisted on a mass election where citizens cannot deliberate and in which control of such discussion as there is passes to the mass media.[5] Local party organizations and elites may have been discomfited, but at the cost of increasing the sway of far more powerful and less accessible elites, as Henry Jones Ford forecast long ago.[6] More of us vote in primaries, but our voices are not heard, and our vote says little about what we think, feel, and revere. Adding insult to injury, the primary system produces candidates who are unworthy. In 1980, voters made clear their distaste for the result; it is now up to their leaders to scrap the process.

Unfortunately, the primaries are probably here to stay. They are suited to liberal political theory, the "irrational Lockeanism" that dominates our thinking about public matters.[7] In liberal theory, human beings are not naturally political animals. They are isolated individuals, concerned to protect themselves and advance their essentially private interests. In this view, we have an interest in deciding who rules us, but no interest in ruling, since rule requires that we take time away from our private concerns.

Self-government becomes government we *choose* rather than government in which we *participate,* and democracy is defined by elections, not deliberation. The primary system, which derives from liberal individualism, is compatible with all the forces that are fragmenting our communities, our political parties, and our public life. At best, we will try to "improve" the primaries, an endeavor that can inspire no confidence. These sadly limited efforts ignore the signs, evident in 1980, of a demand for politics and party government.

The Democrats: The Necessity of Party

For the Democrats, the election of 1980 was their worst defeat in a quarter century. The returns seem unambiguous; the Democratic Party was repudiated by an electorate that decided to "Vote Republican, For a Change." Yet even that statement must be qualified, given the peculiarities of the election.

Toward the end of his campaign, Jimmy Carter appealed more and more to party loyalties and the Democratic pantheon. A Democratic advertisement featured clips of Franklin Roosevelt, Harry Truman, and Jack Kennedy; Lady Bird Johnson and Muriel Humphrey said a few words. It was a celebration of tradition and an appeal to allegiance—and it came entirely too late.

For four years, Carter disdained the party and its organizations. He recognized that party loyalties—and especially, loyalties to party organizations—seemed to be attenuating, and he had no interest in reversing the decline. As Carter apparently saw it, the Democratic Party apparatus was simply a collection of more or less parochial interest groups, committed to inflationary policies and the expansion of the federal bureaucracy and tied to outdated patronage politics. It was part of the "establishment" Carter had opposed in 1976, which for the most part had opposed his nomination. He saw little to hope for from it, and he preferred to build a personal coalition devoted to policies deemed in the public interest, especially as defined by "good management" rather than politics. The personal note was ubiquitous; even the membership organization of the Democratic National Committee called itself "The President's Club."

In the first few months of his administration, Carter initiated a number of highly publicized ventures in direct contact with citizens designed to end the isolation of the Nixon years. He attended a "town meeting"; he answered telephone calls from voters, took notes on their questions, and called back with answers. It was undeniably good politics; the programs were popular, and they enlisted support. Yet they were allowed to lapse. The president evidently thought of them as symbolic gestures, a sort of political fluff to be sacrificed to the real, administrative demands of the presidency. He did not return to the town meeting, for example, until late in his administration.

The president thus scorned party, the traditional basis of support in Congress and the country, but he did not appeal to voters directly in any way sufficiently consistent and compelling to move reluctant members of Congress to his side. Rather halfheartedly, he did invoke the public on behalf of the "windfall profits tax" against the oil lobby, and even that lukewarm appeal contributed to one of the infrequent cases in which his program succeeded. Carter seemed to realize that one cannot successfully appeal to the public very often. He did not recognize, as great presidents always did, that this implies that recourse to the general public is most effective as the exception to a strategy of party government. Party, for all its faults, sometimes *may* move a member of Congress beyond immediate self-interest, which alone is enough to make it invaluable.

We need no encouragement, after all, to be self-interested and parochial. In a country as vast and diverse as the United States, the public interest is a distant abstraction. It may be that it is in my interest to help workers in Youngstown, but the connections that tie my interest to theirs are indirect, impalpable, and subtle. I know, by contrast, that it helps me to pay lower taxes.[8] If you tell me that it is in my interest to pay taxes to support those Ohio workers, I will need persuading. I know, too, that America is a changing, complexly interdependent society that no one fully understands. Even if your reasoning is ingenious, you might be wrong; it might make matters worse to try to help the workers in Youngstown. Moreover, you may not have my best interests at heart. Even presuming that you mean well, you may not understand or care about what matters to me.* Surely, I have done all I can be asked to do if I take care of my own. That, at least, is the way all of us are tempted to reason, and many of us submit. Allegiance, public spirit, and support for the common good are in perennial short supply.

Politics—participation and partisanship—are indispensable means for developing civic spirit. My participation in deliberation enlists my support because it makes me feel less helpless: I contribute to the shaping of decisions instead of simply reacting to events. Political participation involves us in, and teaches us to see, the life of a larger society. For most of us, participation can only be local. But even close to home, we can come to know —and possibly, to trust—the local leaders who carry our voice to larger tribunals. These days, of course, even local participation is the exception, although it could be encouraged, and local party organizations are in disarray. But, for most of us, party still gives us some sort of political identity and defines leaders we can trust, "men like ourselves," who can at least be relied on to share more of our basic values than their opponents. Party is still the safest source of trust between rulers and ruled.[9]

Jimmy Carter did more than spurn party; he seemed to violate that trust. Historically, the Democratic Party has stood for compassion and sympathy, for the refusal to allow human relations to be governed by the requirements of "efficiency" or "sound currency." The party's great rhetoric speaks to that commitment, from Bryan's "Cross of Gold" to Roosevelt's credo that "divine justice weighs the sins of the cold-blooded and the

---

* I have vivid memories of McGovern supporters explaining to devout Catholics that opposition to abortion was not, after all, in their "real" interest.

sins of the warm-hearted in different scales." * Carter's emphasis on management and quasi-monetarist fiscal policies were, at
least, a new departure. In 1976, William Shannon wrote, Carter
was "saying that government can be compassionate but also
skeptical."[10] By 1980, the compassion seemed to have vanished.
On the face of it, Carter had broken with Democratic tradition,
and he needed politics and party in the *conduct of government,*
not merely in campaigns, to persuade voters that he acted out of
necessity and with fidelity to the party's heritage. By campaign
time, it was too late, especially since Ronald Reagan was clearly
a man of warm sympathies. Thomas Jefferson taught that "sentiment, not science" was the source of justice, and whatever else
may be said about his argument, it speaks to democratic politics
in general and the politics of the Democratic Party in particular.[11] Carter, neglecting Jefferson's maxim, helped seal his political doom.

For its part, Congress magnified all of Carter's faults. The
horde of neophytes swept into office by Watergate were not
elected by party organization, and most of them had run ahead
of Carter in 1976. They owed the party little, and the president
less. Carter's failures as a party and legislative leader left all too
many members of Congress disposed to play a lone hand, insist-
ing—with fervor greater than that of the Moral Majority—on
pure liberal ideology or following their favorite interest groups.
It was an exceptionally unproductive Congress, especially given
the energy crisis and our economic troubles. Of course, politically, it is easier to give than to take away, and social justice is a
difficult goal in times of relative scarcity.[12] Even if we are generous on that account, however, Congress's record was barren.

A great many voters detested this Congress, not so much
because it was liberal as because it was obstructive. If only the
Congress had been Republican, Jimmy Carter could have tried
to repeat Harry Truman's campaign against the "obstruc-

---

* The quotation is from Roosevelt's acceptance speech, 27 June
1936: *The Public Papers and Addresses of Franklin D. Roosevelt* (New
York: Random House, 1938), 5:235.

tionists" of the "do-nothing" Eightieth Congress.[13] In this, at least, Carter and the congressional Democrats were united: Carter could not denounce them effectively. What the voters rejected, however, was not the Democratic Party. It was *government without party*, the combination of Carter's managerialism and the Congress's indiscipline. That makes it harder than it ought to be to read the party currents in 1980.

The New Deal Coalition and the New Deal Family

Political parties are not ad hoc coalitions of interest groups for and against particular policies, going out of being as quickly as they appear. Parties make deeper claims on our memories, our identities, and our hopes. In many ways, a party is like a family. New members are added; some old members are lost to new connections; some kinsmen become distant, while others, who have been out of touch, come back into the family circle. With those rare exceptions called "critical elections," parties undergo "slow, all but unconscious transformation."[14] The election of 1980 suggests that the New Deal coalition is no longer with us; but, to this moment at least, the New Deal family is still alive, its relationships strained and altered but still intact.

In 1932, Franklin Roosevelt inherited a political party in which the southern (and western) wing, Protestant and rural, had lost control to an urban, industrial wing, heavily Catholic and rooted in the Northeast.[15] The change was formally ratified in 1936 with the repeal of the "two-thirds" rule that had allowed the South to block any unacceptable candidate. The New Deal coalition picked up support as it went along—notably from Jews and blacks—but its center of gravity continued to lie with the northern white working class, increasingly unionized and composed of predominantly Catholic ethnic communities. John Kennedy's nomination and victory in 1960 relied on those voters, and it reaffirmed their Democratic allegiance.

Nevertheless, two gradual processes were changing the

Democratic coalition. The first was obvious: Those who profited from the New Deal developed new economic interests. Protected by trade unions, contracts, seniority, and pension rights,
established workers had less to fear from unemployment and
more to fear from inflation. Given the entitlements of this ex-
panding "contract society," old anxieties were pushed into the
background. Established workers became homeowners worried
about property taxes and parents concerned with the costs of
higher education. Moving into middle-class styles of life, sometimes at great cost, they felt menaced by affirmative action programs that seemed to threaten their own—and even more, their
children's—ascent and which undermined the neighborhood
school. A variety of new economic and social interests strained
the old ties of established workers to the Democratic Party.

On the whole, however, white ethnic workers remained
loyal to the party. Their memories of the past ran too strong,
and Republican hostility to their gains was too apparent. The
"right to work" crusade by Republican hard-liners in 1958, for
example, revitalized Democratic loyalties that had begun to wa-
ver in the 1950s. The white working-class communities stayed
in the Democratic coalition, but they became increasingly exposed to cross-pressures, propertied proletarians who were vulnerable to issues like "communism in government" or, more recently, the "social issue."[16]

These ethnic working-class communities, the backbone of
"regular" Democratic Party organizations, became increasingly
unreliable. The regulars became irregular, undependable voters;
"safe" districts, in state or national elections, changed into the
arenas of interparty competition. It has been years since the
Democratic Party could take these voters for granted, and holding them in the coalition requires increasing attention to their
dignity, their particular concerns, and their sense of neglect.[17]

As white working-class Democrats ceased to be the core of
the party's support, blacks replaced them. Increasingly, blacks
are the "new Irish," the party regulars and the heart of Democratic straight-ticket support. Carter held black voters in 1980

and may even have increased his support marginally. In fact, Carter's achievement, in 1976, in bringing the South back into the Democratic fold was possible only because of monolithic support from southern blacks. The relatively high Democratic totals in the South in 1980 reflect Carter's own residual regional popularity, but they also reflect the comparatively large number of black voters. It is not merely a quixotic passion that made Senator Strom Thurmond speak, in the aftermath of Reagan's victory, of "reexamining" the Voting Rights Act of 1965. As long as that act remains in effect, a Democratic South is likely whenever the region's interests and feelings are reasonably reflected in the Democratic platform and nominee.*

The fact that blacks have displaced the white working class as the party's regulars, however, is an indication of shifts that have taken place in the Democratic coalition. The blacks have moved to the core; the white ethnics have moved to the periphery; the pattern of urban residence is replicated in party loyalty. This, by any standard, is a change from the old relationships of the New Deal.

In that sense, the Roosevelt coalition has come to an end, as it was bound to. There are middle-aged voters today who were not born when Franklin Roosevelt died, and the youngest voters in 1980 were only a year old when John Kennedy was shot. We will remember Roosevelt and the Great Depression less and less, and—just as Truman has suddenly acquired cachet—Kennedy will increasingly be the symbol whose memory excites Democratic partisans.

There are strong tactical reasons for that change of symbols. Democrats need to give unmistakable evidence, as Kennedy's campaign did in 1960, of their concern for white workers and ethnic Americans. Notably, no Catholic has received the Democratic nomination since Kennedy, despite a sharp rise in

---

* An extraordinary amount of this is anticipated in V.O. Key, "The Future of the Democratic Party," *Virginia Quarterly* 28 (1952): 161–75; see also Donald Matthews and James Prothro, *Negroes and the New Southern Politics* (New York: Harcourt Brace Jovanovich, 1966).

ethnic consciousness. Senator Edward Kennedy might have won the nomination in 1980, in fact, if he had been less identified with liberalism and more identified with his ethnic heritage. Attending to the dignity and the concerns of working-class, ethnic audiences must be a Democratic priority. In 1976, William Shannon thought that Carter was "tacitly repositioning his party" to achieve that goal, especially through his concern for "patriotism, a strengthening of families and neighborhoods, and the work ethic."[18] Carter's failure to develop these themes ranks high among the political failures of his administration.

Certainly, Democrats need to be concerned that working-class America be better represented in party councils and that the party give less attention, by contrast, to advocates of abortion rights, gay liberation, and similar movements, who have —given the logic of American politics—nowhere else to go except into third-party impotence. The Democrats have one tactical advantage. When they lose an election, the defeated candidates tend to be drawn from the party's extreme liberal wing, as were so many of this year's losers. Defeat can contain its own corrective, driving the party back to more pragmatic bastions. But that remains to be seen.

A final note is needed. Foreign policy strained the Democratic coalition as severely, in 1980, as the tensions inherent in the "contract society." Even among those voters who remember FDR, memories of World War II, the common experience of older and middle-aged voters, have grown more important as recollections of the depression wane. The war years created a deep sense of American power, and everything in the early postwar years strengthened that impression. For all but the youngest voters, American power and independence are basic expectations and fundamental assumptions rooted deep in the emotions. The "decline" of American power has, correspondingly, been both painful and fundamentally incomprehensible.

Since American postwar power depended, in part, on the prostrate condition of Europe and Japan, the decline of our position was predictable. Moreover, declining or no, America is still a colossus. Nevertheless, one does not "reason" with basic feelings. We grew up with the sense that America did not depend on anyone. We were genuinely independent, an "arsenal of democracy" capable, if the need arose, of going it alone. In large measure, these feelings were justified at the time: our only major shortage during World War II was rubber, and we rationed gasoline to save tires. Even during the Arab oil boycott of 1973, we were relatively unaffected and could have taken a high tone if we wished. In recent years, by contrast, we have been forced to deal with the reality of our dependence on others. We need the Saudis to keep the oil flowing at premium prices; we need the Germans to support the dollar; we must listen to both hector us about the need to control inflation. And so on. It does not help much to remind ourselves that other countries need us as much as we need them. The experience of dependence is painful, even if it is shared. In 1980, Steven Roberts observed, we were brought face-to-face with "America, the vulnerable."[19]

The prolonged conflict of America and Iran over the hostages reminded us of all the things we could *not* do, all the constraints and reasons for inaction. Reagan touched a deep chord when he said that, if elected, he would not "do nothing," as Carter had done. Raised in an activist culture, we believe that people can master nature and that civilization can rise above barbarism. Yet our helicopters broke down in the Iranian desert, and there was the Ayatollah, barbarism incarnate, and the crowds chanting, "Khomeini fights, Carter trembles." We *felt* it as a "humiliation," the word Reagan used, and Iran, along with any number of slights and setbacks, readied us for heroic measures in foreign policy. As Richard Betts wrote:

In the 1970s ... "No more Vietnams" became as misleading and confining a principle as "no more Munichs.".... Today, the pendulum is swinging back. Soviet advances in Ethiopia, Afghanistan and Yemen and the collapse of the regime in Teheran, raise the specter of falling dominos. Hysterical reaffirmation of containment by large-scale intervention will be no improvement over adamant abstention.[20]

Betts is probably right, but the mood is unmistakable.

I suspect that we are ready for similarly drastic remedies in domestic affairs, where they may be more clearly needed. The voters do not want a nine-to-five regime that leaves them alone. They selected Reagan partly in the hope that he would prove a "strong leader," and a majority would probably welcome declaration of an "economic state of emergency." Of course, Americans are not eager for constraint and sacrifice. They may be ready for policies that suggest strong action and to which citizens can *contribute*.

President Carter's policies relied on indirect government controls, such as the effort to curb inflation through rising interest rates or the more successful attempt to limit gasoline consumption by allowing prices to rise. Such policies, however, make citizens feel helpless, whether or not they are successful. We are allowed only to react to events. Even when such policies work, we feel we are being manipulated, and all too often we suspect that these policies distribute sacrifice unfairly. Direct controls—gas rationing, for example—are more compatible with our dignity and with our concern for justice. They ask for conscious sacrifice for a public purpose, with the burden distributed on the basis of public criteria. And whatever their other problems, direct controls are more likely to make us feel that our problems can be solved by political action.

Certainly, there is no need for the Democrats to retreat from their commitment to "big government." They should, of course, suggest that they would manage government efficiently, and they need to demonstrate an increased concern for local community. But there is a good deal of reason to believe that, in foreign and domestic policy, many voters who defected to Reagan wanted *more* government, not less, and that they chose him hoping for a regime that would be less hesitant and ambivalent about the use of power. The Roosevelt coalition is passing, and the Kennedy coalition may be succeeding it within the New Deal family. That ought to hint, at least, at nostalgia for Camelot; imperial government may be on the verge of a new wave of popularity.

The Republicans and the New Conservatives

It was surely a sign of the times that the Republican candidate, by his own admission, voted for Roosevelt all four times he ran.*

One of Reagan's undoubted advantages was his freedom from the baggage of old-line Republicanism. He quoted Roosevelt happily; he paraded his admittedly peculiar trade-union past and his lifetime membership in the Screen Actors Guild. Even his attacks on the cherished gains of labor—his criticism of the minimum wage, for example—were couched in language designed to make them acceptable. Reagan argued for a "two-tier" wage system, with a lower minimum wage for teen-agers and the hard-core unemployed. Whatever else may be said of this proposal, it was tailored to allay the fears of established white workers. Reagan preferred to run as a New Dealer grown conservative, and that stance persuaded millions of voters that he was safe enough to afford them the luxury of dumping Carter.

Reagan's campaign, in other words, signals changes in conservatism more striking than any change in the Democratic majority. Not so long ago, Reagan's rhetorical fondness for organized labor would have been high treason in Republican circles. The "supply-side" economics symbolized by the Kemp-Roth tax proposal, moreover, indicates the change even more clearly. Traditional Republican doctrine always worried about inflation. True to laissez-faire, it wanted to let the market alone and relied

---

* Reagan also voted for Truman, apparently; John Connally, of course, voted Democratic as late as 1968, but he, evidently, is still regarded as a turncoat.

heavily on the "bourgeois virtues" of the independent middle class. The cure for inflation, in this doctrine, was less consumption and more saving, self-discipline, and frugality. Asked the cure for rising food prices in 1947, Senator Robert A. Taft responded, "We should eat less."[21] Nothing could have been more alien to the style and substance of Reagan's campaign, and Reagan made much, scornfully, of Carter's suggestion that inflation resulted from the fact that we have lived "too well." Rectitude and self-denial were themes of Congressman Anderson's campaign, but Anderson's old-style, middle-class individualism is now peripheral in Republican politics.

Reagan's proposals turn on the notion that less restraint—a massive tax cut—can stimulate investment and productivity enough to offset inflation. Self-indulgence takes the place of self-denial. After years of learning that "you don't shoot Santa Claus," the Republicans decided to nominate him. Even if Reagan's proposals work as well as he hopes, they make a mockery of middle-class virtues. Ants are only grim, ill-humored folks who eat badly; grasshoppers are good citizens who fight inflation too. Supply-side economics is self-consciously modeled on the Kennedy tax cut of 1963, and it clearly involves government planning, though planning of a decidedly conservative sort.

In fact, a good many of Reagan's promises suggest more government intervention, not less. During the campaign, for example, he argued for "enterprise zones" to stimulate growth in the industrial cities, and his transition team circulated a paper that would deny federal aid to any locality that persisted in rent control. These are conservative plans, but they call for a good deal of government involvement on behalf of the "private sector." And all this says nothing about Reagan's proposals for stronger defense and federal policies to defend the family.

In fact, the term "private sector" is a talisman. In the first place, it suggests that there is a legitimate *public* sector, an inescapable component of government input into and regulation of our economic life. In the second place, referring to the "private sector" allows Reagan to scrap "free enterprise" with its laissez-faire connotations. Like quoting Roosevelt, referring to the "private sector" is a way of disowning the past, abandoning the world of the independent, small-town bourgeoisie for the new world of tax shelters, multinationals, and computer programs, where planning is the rule.

Reagan suggests that the private sector, assisted by a sympathetic government, can make sacrifice unnecessary. We are an "energy-rich" country, and the energy companies will prove it. Taxing ourselves less will still enable us to balance the budget and provide for a bigger military, and at the same time interest rates will come down. Reagan, in other words, presents himself as the defender of the American "fifth freedom," the *right to consume,* and he assures us that we will enjoy that liberty in his term of office.

It is hard to say how much of this the voters believed. Carter took a more somber tone, but he also shied away from any call for self-denial, promising "careful" and "balanced" tax cuts and the like. Voters, in other words, were neither asked nor permitted to choose between austerity and extravagance. Anderson's "new realism" seems the exception to this rule, since he did not hesitate to call for restraint. With few exceptions, however, Anderson's supporters knew he would not win; they knew, in other words, that in practice they would not be required to *make* the sacrifices he urged. His candidacy, therefore, had a secret attraction for well-to-do liberals. Since in practice, a vote for Anderson helped elect Reagan, his supporters could affirm their anti-inflationary *principles* at the same time that they forwarded their inflationary *desires.* In any case, it seems likely that a great many of Reagan's supporters took their candidate's economics with a grain of salt.

It is hard to believe, for example, that a great many voters did not notice that Reagan's faith in the private sector was contradicted by Detroit's dramatic, dismal failure to anticipate the demand for small, fuel-economical cars. In reality, the auto industry showed all the rigidity and lack of imagination that, in conservative doctrine, is supposed to characterize government. The auto industry underrated the need to economize and our willingness to do so; the federal government, by contrast, had been urging the change on a recalcitrant Detroit for some time. The example of the auto industry does not augur well for a policy of "getting the government off the backs of the American people." Detroit will need more help, not less, and the new conservatives will probably provide it. The private sector does not want to be let alone; it wants government to help it and, where necessary, to pick up the tab. In economics, that is likely to be the direction of the new regime.

A good many Democrats who defected to Reagan ignored his economics. They voted for him in the hope that he will do something about the "social issue," introducing government into the world of the family and the other traditional refuges of private life. Clearly, this calls for "big government" with a vengeance, and while the social issue was bound to hurt any Democratic regime, the new Republican administration is not likely to find it much more congenial.

Americans continued to feel society crumbling around them in 1980. Carter had promised to make the American family a major concern of his administration, but the Democrats only damaged themselves when they tried to address the issue. Civil libertarians and partisans of new, "liberated" arrangements protested against making the traditional family the norm of policy, and the administration yielded, although it ought to have been possible to advocate stronger and more stable relationships whether or not these are "traditional." Fundamentalists expected more from Carter than Sunday pieties, and they did not get it. And while Carter himself was against providing federal funds for abortion—little enough to ask, as "right-to-lifers" saw it—the Democratic convention in New York decidedly did not share the president's view.

Reagan made every effort to appeal to social conservatives, especially since the social issue lies at the hiatus between the liberals and working-class Democrats. There is little doubt that

Reagan's administration will continue this strategy, and the new president can be relied on to oppose the ERA and abortion, to look for ways to permit prayer in the schools, and possibly to support aid to denominational education.

There is every reason, however, to think that Reagan's social conservatism, though sincere, is also superficial. The forces that are weakening local communities and families are bound up with our individualism, mobility, and commitment to growth. Change, "unsteady, irregular and hard to predict" makes yesterday's certainties into today's follies.[22] We cannot commit ourselves very deeply to the institutions that are so prone to change; and people, like everything else, are only too likely to be different tomorrow.* Children, uprooted from homes and neighborhoods, learn through loss to be more reserved in making their commitments. People who are left behind—so often the old—frequently suffer even more than those who leave, and become still more guarded in consequence. Long-distance may be "the next best thing to being there," but AT&T is only reminding us that we will probably *not* live close to our families or old friends. Our communities, as Scott Greer wrote years ago, are "limited liability communities" where we learn to commit ourselves only superficially, retaining the freedom to cut our losses or move up as the social market dictates.[23]

Family relationships are bound to reflect these currents. We have learned more and more to regard divorce as a normal event of life. The election of Reagan, the first divorced person to become president, will probably do more to legitimate divorce than his conservatism will do to stabilize families. Yet the more normal divorce seems, the more we are reminded that we can and do make mistakes in judging others, even in our most important commitments and in our strongest feelings. And thus the more we are likely to limit our subsequent commitments. Herbert

---

* I find it illustrative that in our tax code, *six months* is a "long term" for the purpose of assessing capital gains. (*Since I wrote this, reforms have changed the holding period to one year, but this does not weaken the basic point.*—Author note, 1995.)

Hendin writes that affection and harmony are growing scarcer, "in and out of families." We are drawing more and more into ourselves and away from family, country, and community.[24]

Reagan is not likely to lend federal power to the quest for stability in personal relationships. To do so, however indirectly, would require a willingness to curb individual freedom, change, and economic growth; but both Republican ideology and the corporate economy regard such restraint as anathema. To make family, community, and morality the goals of public policy would require that we subordinate private liberty to civil order, something neither Reagan nor his party is likely to consider. As Reagan's ambassador to the United Nations, Jeane Kirkpatrick, wrote in 1979,

> Republican spokesmen have consistently emphasized private concerns such as profit and taxes, and private virtues such as self-discipline and self-reliance and either have not had, or have not communicated, a persuasive conception of the public good.[25]

The reason is simple: the tradition of liberal individualism, which shapes Republican ideology, acknowledges no public good that is not simply an aggregate of private goods and liberties. Reagan will give social conservatives the symbols, but he will leave the substance to the forces that are making for privatism and social disintegration. If there is light and hope in the future of the Republic, it is not visible in the election of 1980.

Notes

1. Irwin Ross, *The Loneliest Campaign* (New York: New American Library, 1969), 35–57.
2. Plato, *Republic,* bk. I, 347B–D.

3. Austin Ranney, "The Representativeness of Primary Electorates," *Midwest Journal of Political Science* 12 (1968): 224–38.

4. James Ceaser, "America's Primaries: Part of the Problem or Part of the Solution?" *Los Angeles Times,* 8 June 1980.

5. Walter Nicgorski, "The New Federalism and Direct Popular Election," *Review of Politics* 34 (1972): 3–15.

6. Henry Jones Ford, "The Direct Primary," *North American Review* 190 (1909): 1–14.

7. Louis Hartz, *The Liberal Tradition in America* (New York: Harcourt, Brace, 1955).

8. Mancur Olson, *The Logic of Collective Action* (Cambridge, Mass.: Harvard University Press, 1965).

9. Otto Kirchheimer, "The Party in Mass Society," *World Politics* 10 (1958): 289–94; see also John L. Sullivan and Robert O'Connor, "Electoral Choice and Popular Control of Public Policy," *American Political Science Review* 66 (1972): 1256–68.

10. William V. Shannon, "Liberalism, Old and New," *New York Times,* 2 October 1976, 25.

11. Adrienne Koch and William Peden, eds., *The Life and Selected Writings of Thomas Jefferson* (New York: Modern Library, 1944), 404.

12. Otto Eckstein, "The Economics of the Sixties," *Public Interest* 19 (Spring 1970): 86–97.

13. Ross, *Loneliest Campaign,* 176–80.

14. Matthew Josephson, *The Politicos* (New York: Harcourt, Brace, 1938), 287.

15. David Burner, *The Politics of Provincialism: The Democratic Party in Transition, 1918–1932* (New York: Knopf, 1967); see also Arthur N. Holcombe, *The New Party Politics* (New York: Norton, 1933).

16. Samuel Lubell, *The Revolt of the Moderates* (New York: Harper & Row, 1956) .

17. Daniel P. Moynihan, "Bosses and Reformers," *Commentary* 31 (June 1961): 461–70.

18. Shannon, "Liberalism, Old and New."

19. Steven V. Roberts, "The Year of the Hostage," *New York Times Magazine,* 2 November 1980, 26ff.

20. Richard K. Betts, "From Vietnam to Yemen," *New York Times,* 25 March 1979.

21. Ross, *Loneliest Campaign,* 42.

22. Alvin Toffler, "Law and Order," *Encounter* 41 (July 1973): 19.

23. Scott Greer, *The Emerging City* (New York: Free Press, 1962).

24. Herbert Hendin, *The Age of Sensation* (New York: Norton, 1975); see also Christopher Lasch, *The Culture of Narcissism* (New York: Norton, 1979).

25. Jeane J. Kirkpatrick, "Why We Don't Become Republicans," *Commonsense*, Fall 1979, cited in the *New York Times*, 23 December 1980, A13; see also J. Hitchcock, "The Uses of Tradition," *Review of Politics* 35 (1973): 3–16.

4

Old Virtues, New Magic:
The Election of 1984

I am giddy, expectation whirls me round.
The imaginary relish is so sweet
That it enchants my sense.

—Troilus and Cressida (III, ii)

The election of 1984 was not a season for heroes; it was won by summer soldiers and sunshine patriots. Mr. Reagan was pleased to have it so; repeatedly, his campaign assured Americans that the long night of crisis was over, giving way to a new morning. Reagan proclaimed that America is "back," the Republic of our fonder memories, affluent and powerful, a "shining city" and an Opportunity Society, built of alabaster and free from tears.

American voters recognized the hyperbole in the president's rhetoric. They knew that some Americans are poor—in fact, there are more poor people in every section of the country than there were when Ronald Reagan took office—and a good many Americans worried, fitfully, about the "fairness" of the president's policies, but the great majority did not allow such concerns to be decisive. Unemployment, the great Democratic issue, worried voters more than inflation, but relatively few Americans were disturbed about either. Ronald Reagan was credited with curing inflation and restoring a modest economic confidence, allowing Americans to anticipate well-being even if they did not enjoy it. For many voters, foreign affairs were the area of greatest concern, but the country was at peace, and the things Americans feared, however troubling in prospect, were at least not at hand.[1]

Most Americans knew, or suspected, that the good times would not always be with us.* For a considerable number, in fact, the Reagan recovery probably represented not springtime but Indian summer. Nevertheless, the Americans who gave Ronald Reagan his great victory wanted at least a respite from the politics of crisis and thought they could expect it. Immediately after the election, when the president's forecasts turned bleak and the administration began to speak of tightening belts, Congressman Newt Gingrich (R-Georgia), a leader of the New Right, observed that "the American people have to feel a little like they thought they were walking into the office of a cruise ship and found out they were in a cancer clinic." Conservative Senator James McClure (R-Idaho), summed it up: "There is nothing you can read in the election that says the American people are ready for sacrifice."[2]

There is more than self-interest in the mood of the majority. Tocqueville wrote that American democracy could endure political conflict and the ordeal of change because of the security Americans found in social and moral life. The health of democracy presumes, Tocqueville declared, that moral ties grow stronger as political bonds are relaxed; in America, the political world was "agitated, uncertain and disputed," but the moral world was "classed, adapted, directed and foreseen."[3] The America Tocqueville was describing, of course, was simpler and more uniform, a republic by, if not only for, Protestant white Anglo-Saxons. Uneasily, the United States has been growing more pluralistic ever since. Nevertheless, Americans could rely, until recently, on certain social and moral decencies as stable standards of right, the sources of direction and meaning. "Our

---

* For example, about 70 percent of Americans were convinced, despite the president's protestations, that taxes would have to be raised.

common difficulties," Franklin Roosevelt declared in 1933, "concern, thank God, only material things."[4]

No more: Americans are troubled by social disorganization and moral *dissensus*. The spiritual foundations of the New Deal are at least as eroded as its politics. In 1984, Americans embraced material prosperity, hoping that *it* would provide the basis for social and moral renewal. Like every presidential contest since 1972, the election of 1984 involved a modest mandate to rebuild the private foundations of public life. Some of Ronald Reagan's militant supporters favored an outright counterrevolution to overthrow the legacy of the 1960s, if not the New Deal. More generally, however, Americans were concerned to recover some sense of social and moral order without surrendering any of their material gains or their individual liberties. The majority of Americans are ambivalent, unready to make great social and moral commitments. In the moral and social as well as in the economic world, Americans wanted a moment of relaxation, and Ronald Reagan, campaigning as "Dr. Feelgood," knew better than to prescribe any bitter medicine.

Reagan's victory was so one-sided as to suggest a shift in the balance and composition of American political parties, but here, too, Americans were hesitant. The Republican presiden tial coalition does seem to have acquired considerable stability, and in some locales—especially in the South and among younger voters—there were shifts away from the Democrats. But the Democrats held the House and gained in the Senate. The theory of critical elections presumes that our party loyalties and our political identities are reasonably coherent, consistent, and stable; in this respect, the theory may have become obsolete.[5] The election of 1984 does not indicate a stable change of allegiance so much as the unsettling, for a considerable number of Americans, of *all* political allegiances, a weakening of the bonds between voters and the political system. A new political era is coming to birth, but not necessarily an attractive or a happy one.*

---

* I find it suggestive that James Monroe, running in 1820 as the

Reagan and the Politics of the Electronic Age

The personality and presidency of Ronald Reagan dominate the politics of the 1980s. Reagan has been a more skillful and successful president than most of us expected. In the role of chief of state, Reagan has been the ablest president since Kennedy, carrying out the ceremonial functions of the presidency with considerable grace. He has proved, as we are often reminded, to be a "great communicator," a master of the public presidency in the media age.

From the standpoint of popularity, the Reagan administration had matchless timing. Its worst years were its first, and the very depth of the early recession made the recovery seem even brighter. Jimmy Carter probably finished off his chances for reelection by setting out, in an election year, to cure inflation by means of draconian monetarism; Reagan's administration avoided hard decisions in 1984, until the election was over. He offered us the easy life, not blood and toil, and the results speak for themselves.

Yet Reagan's landslide victory was a mixed blessing for his party. Reagan ran as a moderate candidate, a fact that helped to move the Republicans—in popular perception—closer to the center of American politics. But Reagan virtually portrayed himself as a mainstream Democrat: At the Republican convention, the band played the New Deal anthem, "Happy Days Are Here Again"; Reagan quoted Roosevelt, Truman, and Kennedy to the exclusion of Republicans; his campaign even traveled on Truman's whistle-stop train. Reagan went beyond simple symbols: he embraced programs and policies that, until recently, were considered left of center; he justified mountainous deficits, pledged not to cut present or future entitlements to Social Security, and voiced support for Medicare.* It helped that Walter

---

architect of the Era of Good Feeling, won a victory even more one-sided than Reagan's, and his triumph resulted in the death of the old party system and the rise of mass political parties.

    * Even after the election, the administration balanced its sharp cuts in domestic welfare programs—including Medicare—with a sur-

Mondale, encumbered by honor and honesty, was forced to the fiscal right. Mondale felt compelled to offer a plan for reducing the deficit, and even with a tax increase, he was barely able to hold the line on social programs. Mondale had no room for exciting new programs and policies; the deficit, and his attempts to combat it, would have made Mondale seem uninspiring even if he had the tongue of angels.[6]

Moreover, it fell to Mondale to emphasize the limits of federal power on social issues and in foreign policy. The combination of fiscal responsibility and political restraint made Mondale sound vaguely like an old-line Taft Republican.* That fact probably enhanced Mondale's appeal to Anderson Republicans, but those voters are too few in number to add more than moral tone. With Walter Mondale's assistance, Ronald Reagan blurred the old lines.

At the same time, the Republican Party became even more dominated by its conservative wing. At the Republican convention, the key victories were won by the right; during the campaign, Republican moderates suffered notable defeats—Elliot Richardson, for example, lost a senatorial primary in Massachusetts, and Charles Percy was denied reelection—while the most visible champion of the right, Jesse Helms, survived. The Republicans, as a party, were bent on drawing the line between left and right, though, admittedly, a line of a new sort.

The president's strategists smoothly ditched his party. Reagan made campaign appearances to support Republican candidates, especially at the end, but this formal support could not eliminate the disparity between the style of the president's campaign and the stance of Republican candidates. Ronald Reagan, in other words, gave the voters no real reason—much less a sense of urgency—to defeat Democratic candidates for Congress. "Why would somebody vote for President Reagan and then vote for John Kerry?" asked Ray Shamie, the defeated Re-

---

prisingly liberal plan for tax reform.

* On abortion, after all, Mondale was arguing that "you can't legislate morality."

publican nominee for the Senate in Massachusetts. "It doesn't make any sense."[7] But a great deal of Mr. Reagan's campaign was devoted to telling voters, implicitly, that it did make *sense,* even if it was not the choice the president would *prefer.* Had his strategists charted a more partisan campaign, Reagan might have lost another half dozen states, but he might also have won a working majority in Congress. In the end, the public voted for Ronald Reagan for the same reason that it voted the Democrats back into control of the House and strengthened their position in the Senate: it desires no great change.[8]

All through the campaign, the Democrats were daunted by Reagan's mastery of television, as they had been ever since he took office. The president reads a speech extremely well, and his humor—especially, his gift for goodspirited self-deprecation—covers many faults. Even the president's intellectual limitations help: Nixon was too shrewd not to *know* when he was being evasive, distorting the facts or contradicting some earlier position, and it showed; Reagan reads his lines innocently and with evident sincerity. The Democratic candidates were not in Reagan's league; only Jesse Jackson had forensic talent, and Jackson's rhetoric is suited more to the pulpit than the screen.

The Democrats' disdavantage, however, was due only in part to the idiosyncrasies of their candidates; it has something to do with their party. The Democratic Party in 1984 was still rooted in an older political science and political practice, the pluralistic doctrine that formed the basis of "interest group liberalism."[9] Too many of the leaders of the party—and most notably, its intellectual leaders—failed to recognize the new shape of political society. In 1984, the Democrats were brought face to face with the inadequacy of the public philosophy that succeeded the era of the New Deal.

Pluralistic doctrine plays down the importance of public speech. In line with the traditional assumptions of American political practice, pluralistic political science assumes that speech is *mediated*—that what candidates say passes to voters through "gatekeepers" such as interest groups, local party organizations, and the press in a "two-step flow of communication."[10] In this view, the public is insulated against the media and against public speech, trusting its gatekeepers enough to let them interpret words and events.

What matters, in this view, is not eloquence but the ability to *do,* and especially the ability to persuade the gatekeepers of one's ability, competence, and force. Adlai Stevenson, consequently, was damned as a "talker," too inclined to play Hamlet, and Humphrey tried vainly to live down his reputation for being "gabby." One's public qualities as a leader, Patrick Caddell observes, are "discounted in Washington, where conviction is less important than the ability to get results."[11] As Caddell implies, Washington insiders are especially likely to esteem leaders who show a mastery of fact, persuasiveness in small and expert groups, and skill in hammering out agreements. Lyndon Johnson and Walter Mondale passed those tests with high marks, and Jimmy Carter—though he failed in many respects—at least aspired to do well.

Ronald Reagan, on the other hand, is not highly regarded —to put it mildly—by the insiders, who tend to be contemptuous of Reagan's superficiality, his administrative weakness, and his too frequent ignorance.[12] Yet the antipathy of the insiders has failed to shake Reagan's appeal to ordinary voters.

In fact, the contemporary public is increasingly without gatekeepers. Local party organizations are in disarray. Even when voters are members of interest groups, they are apt to feel distant and disaffected, as so many trade unionists do. The print media, the citadel of interpretation, have declined in favor of television and other forms of direct access to the public. The shattering of the old structures of mediation confronts the Democrats—and political scientists—with a truth they should not have forgotten: politics is fundamentally a matter of speech, and in democracies, of public speech. But it also confronts America with a public that more and more lacks both the arts of listening and the friendship of critics and guides.

Reagan's staff knows the secrets of campaigning in our

mass society. It recognizes, in the first place, that there are no terrors in the press. Reagan's campaign provided good "logistical support" for reporters, but it denied them any real access to the candidate, just as the White House staff kept news conferences to a minimum. Mondale, by contrast, appeared to enjoy give-and-take with reporters, holding a news conference almost every day.[13]

Despite his age, Ronald Reagan is more contemporary than his rivals because he was shaped by movies and by his career as host of "Death Valley Days": Reagan, in fact, is the first candidate who is genuinely the product of the era of the visual media. All previous candidates—and certainly Walter Mondale—grew up and were formed in the years before television dominated the American scene. Ronald Reagan is part of a *New* Right in precisely this sense. The Old Right was tied to a structure of mediation, the business and professional leaders, the editors, and the Republican officials of small city, small-town America; the New Right relies on television, as Jerry Falwell does, or on direct mail.

Moreover, Ronald Reagan's staff realizes that television can be *dominated*. Since what matters in politics is so often invisible, subtle, and substantive, it will never be well covered by a medium whose hallmarks are visibility, simplification, and a concern with style.* Television can be managed because of its limitations: reporters can comment only in the context of a picture; the medium is impotent without "photo opportunities" and cannot easily resist a story with good visual possibilities. Reagan's strategists exploited those weaknesses with few scruples and great skill. The president's campaign assertions went largely untested and unchallenged; and the candidate was portrayed, pretty much, in the way his managers desired.

---

* Television reporters, despite their array of technological supports, are often embarrassingly bad at covering politics: During an interview intended to introduce Gary Hart to the voters, for example, Roger Mudd seemed fixated on the stylistic question whether Hart was imitating Kennedy. See John Corry, "TV: Coverage of Hart," *New York Times,* 16 March 1984, C24.

In one respect, the election of 1984 approximated George Orwell's imagined totalitarianism. Orwell feared that in the future, political regimes would find it possible to manipulate our memory of the past and thereby control the future. Things have not reached that pass, but the possibility is frighteningly foreseeable.[14] Ronald Reagan and his advisers recognize, intuitively at least, that the public has less and less memory, less ability to organize and to recall the past. The old, organic sources of political remembrance in families and communities are breaking up and are being replaced by television's presentation of time as a series of disjointed moments, each a discrete unit, available for reordering at will.*

Illustratively, Ronald Reagan maintained that, in 1981, he inherited a "mess" that was the work, over many years, of his Democratic opponents. Yet Republican presidents held office from 1969 to 1977; just as Reagan attempted to enlist Roosevelt, Truman, and Kennedy, he created the sense that Nixon and Ford somehow counted among the Democrats.† One might pass this off as campaign cunning were it not clear that Reagan's own version of history is strikingly disordered; his memories are intertwined with odd fantasies and with bits drawn from old movies, all recalled and related as *fact*. This is an old pattern with Reagan, not a sign of age. He is, in this as in other things, a very modern man, one for whom history is not an objective past but an existential creation, the product of will.‡

---

   * We are, after all, on the political eve of TV's second generation—children raised by parents who themselves grew up in the era of television.

   † By contrast, when Roosevelt spoke of "inheriting a mess" in 1933, the Republicans had held office for 24 of the 32 preceding years; in the 32 years before Reagan took office, Republicans and Democrats had each held office for 16.

   ‡ Michael Rogin's Gauss lecture, "Reagan, the Movie," at Princeton University in 1984 develops this theme in a matchless way. See also Gwinn Owens, "Reagan's Confusion of Fact and Fantasy Raises Doubts about Future Competency," *New Brunswick Home News*, 26 March 1984, B7.

LEADERSHIP: OLD VALUES AND NEW AMERICA

Ronald Reagan's reputation as a "strong leader" is his greatest political asset, and the quality of his leadership—so generally admired by the electorate—reveals a good deal about the state of America as a political society.

In speech, Reagan is almost invariably firm and decisive, certain of his values and his direction, and inclined to strong language and striking expression. In action, Reagan often wavers and vacillates. In relation to Lebanon, for example, Reagan denounced those who were ready to "cut and run" and proclaimed his own unwillingness to "surrender," only to order the withdrawal of American forces. William V. Shannon was led to write that, in foreign affairs, there is "no knowledge, no understanding and no commitment in anything that Reagan does."[15] Yet at each muddled stage of the imbroglio in Lebanon, including our eventual retreat—the president called it a "redeployment"—Reagan exuded confidence and proclaimed success. In domestic affairs, the president's defeats have been less dramatic and less frequent, but his pragmatic flexibility has been just as evident.

Reagan suits our mood. Americans, for the most part, want a leader who gives us a sense of direction and moral purpose, but not one who really *does* dangerous or demanding things. It is significant that Reagan flatters us outrageously; in his rhetoric, the American people are sinned against but never sinners. Following Reagan's lead, George Bush denounced Jimmy Carter's famous reference to a national "crisis of confidence" because Carter had "blamed the American people." In 1984, at least, Reagan's leadership combined the language of moral purpose with the practice of social and moral complacency.

The president's vulnerabilities, which his critics expect to bring disaster, only endear him to his audience. Americans know that Reagan is not brilliant, that his command of facts is uncertain, and that he is prone to "gaffes," but they excuse and indulge such evidences of fallibility. As Philip Rieff pointed out, in the symbolism of modern politics, political leaders—especially in mass democratic states—cannot afford to be too superior to their constituents. A leader must be one of us, an ordinary citizen glorified, and consequently must have faults. Reagan's mistakes, in fact, enable citizens to feel protective toward the president.*

Reagan's particular weaknesses, however, say something about our times. Franklin Roosevelt's weaknesses were physical, like the material problems of the country he governed. Spiritually, Roosevelt seemed to tower; even those, like Justice Holmes, who found his intellect second-rate, conceded that FDR had a first-class temperament. Roosevelt was great-spirited in a way that Ronald Reagan is not. Reagan, on the other hand, vaunts his physical vitalities; in 1984, he delighted in his prowess at arm wrestling. By contrast, he shies away from the political "brain wrestling" with the press at which Roosevelt was a past master. Reagan's vulnerabilities, as the voters have every reason to know, are defects of mind and spirit, suited to a country that is troubled in its soul.

The president celebrates traditional values and symbols, but he understands American ambivalence. As a people, Americans suffer from moral uncertainty and spiritual hunger, and they feel and show considerable nostalgia for the old verities and social landmarks. But most Americans do not want to return to the old order; they prefer life in the cities or suburbs, they have grown accustomed to a second income in the family, and they enjoy a certain amount of liberation and latitude in their personal lives. The public has its moments of guilt and regret, but it is unwilling to live by the old ways.

---

* Philip Rieff, "Aesthetic Functions in Modem Politics," *World Politics* 5 (1953): 478–502; this protectiveness extends, with better reason, to the president's staff. Given Reagan's disinterest in policy analysis or administrative detail, his staff—by insulating the president and controlling the information he gets—has a more than usual ability to maneuver Reagan, provided they respect his traditional beliefs, since Reagan is unlikely to seek additional information on his own. David Broder, "Shielding Reagan," *Boston Globe,* 14 October 1984, A23.

A television commercial portrays a young man returning for a celebration at the family farm, intoning that "America's coming home to the good taste of butter," but we know that whatever eating habits the young man takes away, he will not *stay* on the farm. A second commercial shows a farm mother gratified because a son who did *not* return for the family get-together sent a van full of appliances in his stead. These and similar commercials almost exactly parallel the "upbeat" advertising of Reagan's campaign, with its suggestion that economic growth is sufficient homage to the old virtues.

Reagan recognizes that Americans want standards set and meanings affirmed, and that they expect traditional beliefs to be shown respect. At the same time, the president realizes that this creed, like his own, is a *civil* religion, devoted to America as a political society rather than to the God of judgment.* Reagan gave his evangelical and socially conservative allies little more than symbolic support during his first term, allowing their legislative program to languish, and he is not apt to do more in his second four years.

In relation to moral values and social institutions, Walter Mondale was again the victim of his own virtues. Mondale is visibly a man of the old order. His ideas and programs may look to the future—and a surprisingly large number of voters saw Mondale as a man of vision—but his relationships and affects seem to point to the past. His marriage, for example, is apparently stable and happy and, hence, is one with which few contemporary Americans can identify. Gary Hart's marriage, by contrast, amounted to a contemporary soap opera, full of storm, stress, and separation leading to a happy ending. Simi-

---

* "Mr. Reagan's Civil Religion," *Commonweal* 111 (21 September 1984): 483–85; despite his evangelical support, Reagan's own theological comments are likely to be remarkably latitudinarian: "Everyone can make his own interpretation of the Bible," Reagan observed, "and many individuals have been making different interpretations for a long time." Cited in Leo P. Ribuffo, *The Old Christian Right* (Philadelphia: Temple University Press, 1983), 268.

larly, Ronald Reagan's family troubles—his divorce and remarriage, his estrangement from his older son, even his failure to meet his infant grandchild—all make him someone we imagine to be like ourselves, able to understand our hopes and pains. Mondale's undisturbed monogamy was, symbolically, at least as out of date as the brand of politics Tip O'Neill seemed to personify. And to make matters worse, Mondale told us that we had to choose between our decencies and our comforts; most Americans preferred the president's happy discovery that it is possible, after all, to serve both God and mammon.

Reagan also understands the ordinary citizen's sense of grievance against the federal government, the conviction that complex government works to the advantage of the powerful and clever, who understand the loopholes of law and the workings of power. Reagan has usurped the Democrats' role as spokesman for many of America's outsiders. In an important sense, Reagan has reaped where the liberals and the New Left sowed.[16] The critique of American policy in Vietnam and the exposures surrounding Watergate worked, for a time, to the advantage of the liberals and the left, discomfiting their immediate enemies. But the attack on public authority also had the effect of undermining confidence in the federal government as a whole, calling its benevolence into question as much as its competence.

The mood to which Reagan appeals is alienated rather than conservative, more suspicious than committed. A great many voters, obviously, have responded to Reagan's pledge to "get the government off the backs of the American people." That response, however, is not born out of confidence in one's ability to go it alone—Americans know their private indignities too well for that—but out of distrust of the federal government as a champion.

In 1984, Ronald Reagan claimed to have restored America's belief in progress, her secular faith in the future. For Reagan, the old sense of possibility is very much alive, and he speaks of extending prosperity to the poor and developing a

"Star Wars" defense against nuclear attack. Reagan remains convinced that human beings can master nature and that, in the president's favorite quotation from Tom Paine, "We have it in our power to begin the world over again." *

The public's response was overwhelmingly positive, but it was also cautious and restrained. Despite the vogue of optimism, only 23 percent of Reagan's voters cited his "vision of the future" as a reason for their support.[17] The public seems wary of high hopes; Reagan received a vote of thanks for the present more than a mandate for the future. The great majority of Americans voted for Reagan because, with the country at peace, they were ready to answer "Yes" to the question, "Are you better off now than you were four years ago?"

Most Americans appear to be moved by the president's words, but they are content in practice with a scaled-down prosperity and patriotism, tailored to an age of lowered expectations. The experience of the 1970s taught us something about America's limitations and vulnerabilities. In 1984, the majority of Americans were content to overlook the poor and happy to settle for Grenada—a small-scale victory won at low cost. The prevailing opinion is satisfied with an America that is neither heroic nor beautiful, but one that preserves—for most of us—our private comforts and decencies. Reagan has not drawn us together; he has assured us that public life is unnecessary and that we can, safely and in good conscience, confine ourselves to our separate private interests and existences.

Reagan and America are likely to need less anemic loyalties. Looming economic problems are all around us. The federal deficit is now growing faster than the rate of growth in the gross national product, and the increased interest on the federal debt exceeds all of the cuts in domestic spending effected during Reagan's first term. Even that well-publicized public indebtedness pales when compared with our *private* debt, now growing at

---

    * This assertion of Paine's is part of an argument that is radically hostile to the teachings of revealed religion; that Reagan uses it so often is an indication of his own civil religion.

about $300 billion a year.[18] Debt has become an economic way of life. When, during his debate with Geraldine Ferraro, Vice-President Bush sought to dramatize inflation under Carter, he did not refer to the high price of goods but to the high cost of *borrowing* ("21 percent interest rates!"). In fact, Americans are outspending their earnings at the rate of about 10 percent a year, an inflationary pressure held in check so far only by an overvalued dollar and cheap imported goods. In the 1960s, the United States borrowed abroad to finance investment; in the 1980s, we have been borrowing to finance consumption.*

In the workplace, Americans who were reemployed after the recession now work, on the whole, for smaller paychecks. Moreover, the growing sector of the job market offers only low-status work, often temporary, requiring little skill and offering low pay and benefits.[19]

Economically, the administration and the country have been living on borrowed time as well as borrowed money. Threats in foreign policy and the erosion of our social institutions only reinforce the moral that a government devoted to private comforts and dedicated to leaving us alone is not adequate to the problems we face. In that truth, the Democrats may find their opportunity, if they are equal to it.

The Democratic Prospect

For the Democrats in 1984, the primary process—as usual —was divisive, exhausting, and inclined to emphasize the role of ideological activists, organized interests, and, in states with open primaries, voters from outside the party's ranks. Mondale, the winner, was as disgusted as the losers. Nevertheless, the Democrats are not likely to make any major changes for the bet-

---

* Ashby Bladen, "The Acid Test," *Forbes* 134 (17 December 1984): 245; in fact, taking into account the stabilization of oil prices, there has been little decline in inflation under Reagan; see Robert Levine's letter to the *New York Times*, 17 September 1984, A18.

ter; the "Fairness Commission," promised to placate Senator Hart, Jesse Jackson, and their supporters, easily could make matters worse. Modest improvements are possible, but the voters have grown accustomed to the system and the Democrats will have to make the best of it, enjoying what promises to be a Republican donnybrook in 1988. In any case, the Democrats have more fundamental problems.

THE NEW DEAL COALITION AND THE NEW DEAL STRATEGY

After the election, the *New York Times,* while urging a new Democratic agenda, observed that Mondale had won substantial majorities among racial minorities, Jews, trade unionists, big-city residents, and the unemployed, and concluded that "the old New Deal coalition ... remains very much alive."[20] The *Times'* prescription for the Democrats makes sense, but its political history is in error, and that mistake says a great deal about the failure of the Democrats in presidential politics.

The New Deal *coalition*—the majorities that four times elected FDR—began with the Democratic Party that Roosevelt inherited, a party built around southern whites and northern Catholics, the latter providing the crucial base of the urban Democratic organizations. The New Deal *strategy* took both groups more or less for granted, and it set out to add enough votes to create a national majority. New Deal tacticians, consequently, courted liberals (in those days, more likely to call themselves "Progressives"), Jews, the unions and—half-incidentally—blacks and racial minorities.

Like any such strategy, the New Deal's political design gave special attention to the groups it aimed to win. In the event, the New Deal strategy attuned Democrats to the values and sensibilities of the target groups and made the party increasingly tone deaf, if not hostile, to the sensitivities of Catholics and southern whites. In order to hold the New Deal coalition together, Democratic strategists relied on historic loyalties, on the power of the urban party organizations, and on an appeal to the economic interests of all those who benefited from New Deal programs —the poor and the working class, of course, but also protected groups like subsidized southern farmers.

Loyalties and memories erode with time. Even while Roosevelt was alive, southern conservatives grew restive. In 1944, an anti-Roosevelt ticket, the "Regulars," ran unsuccessfully in Texas, and in 1948 the growing conflict over racial policy erupted in the Dixiecrat revolt that eventually took Strom Thurmond, among others, out of the Democratic Party. Similarly, party organizations grew weaker, partly because of secular changes in American life, but also because of the hostility of liberals, who promoted legislation and party rules designed to weaken or break up the "machines." * Today, party organizations are no more than an interest group—and not always a strong one—in local party politics, much too confined to their own supporters to be able to deliver votes to the national party.[21] In 1984, for example, white Democratic leaders in Chicago made relatively little effort to dissuade their constituents from supporting Reagan; instead, they offered to forgive their friends for such defections and hence to preserve social harmony and local community, if they would vote for Paul Simon, the successful Democratic candidate for the Senate. In doing so, they were probably making the best available bargain, but it indicates the diminished role of the "regulars."

By 1972, Democrats were left, in relation to southern whites and northern Catholics, with a kind of pseudo Marxism, the hope that an appeal to economic interests would prove sufficient to hold voter loyalties. "If we don't have an economic issue for those people," Robert Squier declared in 1984, speaking of "born-again" Christians, "we don't seem to have any issues."[22] As Democrats are acutely aware, the success of their own policies has lifted the majority of such voters at least mar-

---

* See, for example, James Reichley, *The Art of Government* (New York: Fund for the Republic, 1959); or Everett C. Ladd, *Where Have All the Voters Gone? The Fracturing of Political Parties* (New York: Norton, 1978).

ginally out of poverty; as a result, Democrats often feel reduced to waiting for a recession. In any case, Democrats know that economic interests are not a sufficient guarantee of party loyalty. No party leader imagines that the economic ties between lower-class blacks and the Democrats would long survive racial insensitivity, and economic interest in the narrow sense would probably lead liberals to support the Republicans. Political allegiance involves our deepest feelings and our highest aspirations as much as our prosaic needs; in the last analysis, political loyalties are a matter for the soul.

The New Deal strategy has played out, whatever we may think of the prospects for the New Deal coalition. It is exhausted because it has succeeded; the groups the New Dealers courted and cultivated have been *won*. The periphery of the New Deal coalition has become the heart of the Democratic Party and the historic Democratic Party—northern Catholics and southern whites—has moved to the periphery, if it has not been lost to the Democrats altogether. The Democrats need a new strategy—whether they hope to restore the old coalition or to build a new one.

The heart of the new Democratic Party—the liberals, the racial minorities, and the trade unions—so accustomed to being wooed, will have to learn how to do the courting, attending to the values, affects, and dignities of others. And correspondingly, the core Democratic groups will have to adjust to their new position. The unions, the minorities, and the liberals will have to ask which items on their respective agendas they are willing to give up in order to win. It is not easy to break a pattern of institutional sensitivity, especially one a half century old, associated with great names and triumphs and buttressed by ideology. The Democrats may find it impossible. Nevertheless, the electoral logic is obvious.

Liberals, for example, have no place else to go. Given the nature of American national politics, they can choose between the Democrats and the irrelevance of third-party candidacies. It is not even clear that such third parties hurt the Democrats very much: Henry Wallace's Progressive Party in 1948 helped establish Truman as the candidate of the center and freed the Democrats from association with the "extreme left," and while John Anderson's candidacy in 1980 certainly cost the Democrats some votes, it may also have helped to hold some southern and moderate Democrats behind President Carter. Organized liberal groups, moreover, seemed relatively ineffective in the electoral politics of 1984. Feminists—having applied pressure heavy-handedly, making Mondale's selection of Geraldine Ferraro look weaker and less daring than it was—failed to deliver a vote sufficient to support their pretensions. Eastern women did give Mondale and Ferraro a majority, and the Democratic ticket did well among younger, unmarried women, but the majority of women voted for the Republican ticket.[23] In any case, it is not credible that organized feminists, or other groups on the liberal left, will be able to support a Republican candidate in the foreseeable future. Such voters need the Democratic Party at least as much, and possibly more, than it needs them.

Trade unions, similarly, no longer have the ability to play one party against the other. In 1980, Mr. Reagan advertised his terms as president of the Screen Actors' Guild as proof of his sympathy for unions; that argument did not surface in 1984. In fact, Reagan set his administration, and the Republicans, on a firmly antiunion course.* The image of organized labor has become undeservedly negative among voters in general; labor's position of power *within* the Democratic Party is one of its few remaining political assets. Walter Mondale would not have won the nomination without the unions, but the embrace of the AFL-CIO helped tag him as a servant of "special interests." Whether it plays its cards foolishly or well, organized labor will continue to be a major power in the internal politics of the Democratic Party, but given its external vulnerabilities, labor will have to walk more carefully and speak more softly.

---

* The Teamsters Union did endorse Reagan, following its usual Republican habits, but the support probably embarrassed the president, since it was suggested that the Teamsters expected in return a less-than-zealous prosecution of their president, Jackie Presser.

Of all the elements of the Democratic core, Jewish voters—at least, those who are not identifiable liberals—may be the most likely to defect to the Republicans. Democrats will certainly need, consequently, to continue to support Israel, and they have every reason to censure anti-Semitism. Yet the increasing role of right-wing Christians within the Republican Party seems likely to tie Jews more closely to the Democrats. "The group that Jews love to hate most," Milton Himmelfarb remarked, "is the Moral Majority."[24] Even Jewish Democrats, in other words, can probably expect somewhat less solicitude than they have learned to take as their due.

Blacks and Hispanics may find it hardest to accept the restraints entailed by their position at the heart of the Democratic Party. Both groups, after all, still have a long agenda of demands and resentments; poverty and social injustice aside, they have overcome political exclusion only recently, if at all. It is not surprising, consequently, that Jesse Jackson campaigned in 1984 on the premise that blacks should approach the Democrats as outsiders, a pressure group that cannot be "taken for granted." But black officeholders, and a surprisingly large majority of black voters, recognize a stronger commitment and obligation to the party.

In inner cities, the Democratic Party is increasingly dominated by blacks; it is becoming as much "theirs" as it was the preserve of the Irish during their glory days, and blacks have every interest in preserving or building the party's ties to whites. Black voters supported Jackson in the primaries on symbolic grounds but appear to have preferred, on pragmatic grounds, that the eventual Democratic nominee be a candidate with a chance to win. Even more striking, only 4 percent of those who supported Jackson indicated that they would be less likely to vote for Mondale—or less likely to vote—if Jackson did not endorse the Democratic ticket.[25] Democrats, of course, would be unwise to underrate Jackson's strength or the mood of assertiveness among new and younger black voters. By and large, however, blacks are straight-ticket regulars; that fact entitles them to greater representation at the highest levels of the Democratic

Party and may, conceivably, make them willing to share the party's burdens.

There are compensations for the hard core Democrats that may encourage them to make the programmatic and affective sacrifices necessary to build a new presidential coalition. They have become the party's establishment, and for practical purposes, the party is their instrument. It is a sign of the times that Walter Mondale, not so long ago regarded as a left-liberal, was identified in 1984 as a "mainstream" Democrat. Yet just as it is hard to change from being cared for to caring for others, it is difficult to accept responsibility for a political institution. Political adulthood, like personal adulthood, is bittersweet. Whatever their regrets, however, the core Democrats have no alternative if they hope to reestablish a national majority.

OLD FRIENDS: THE HISTORIC DEMOCRATS

The most obvious strategy for the Democrats lies in attempting to win back the estranged elements of the old coalition, voters who, for the most part, still think of themselves as Democrats and vote for the party's local candidates. Since Franklin Roosevelt died, this has amounted to the Democrats' only recipe for success. In the elections since World War II, the Democrats have nominated one Catholic, Kennedy, two candidates from the South, Johnson and Carter, and one, Truman, who came from a border state with southern associations. With the exception of Carter's second try in 1980, all were elected. During the same period, the Democrats five times nominated northern Protestants (Stevenson twice, Humphrey, McGovern, and Mondale); all of them have been defeated. Other factors were at work, of course—no candidate, for example, could have beaten Eisenhower—but the pattern is too suggestive to be ignored.*

---

* Incidentally, the pattern is almost reversed for vice-presidential candidates. During the same period, the Democrats chose four southerners (Barkley, Sparkman, Kefauver, and Johnson) and three Catholics (Muskie, Shriver, and Ferraro); only Barkley and Johnson were on winning tickets. By contrast, both northern Protestants nominated by the

Nevertheless, Democrats should not underestimate the difficulty of reestablishing the old coalition. Even the historic loyalties that still tie so many Catholic and southern voters to the Democrats are a mixed blessing. There is no quarrel more bitter than a family argument. A great many Democrats who grew up thinking of the party as their political home have never recovered from the shock they received in 1972, when they found the national convention filled with strangers and themselves—or people with whom they identified—treated as unwelcome guests. And others have been embittered by what they experience as abandonment and years of neglect.

In 1984, Democrats rested much of their hope on the "fairness issue," the recognition that the burden of Reagan's policies falls disproportionately on poor and low-income Americans. Even more than in 1980, however, the Republicans benefited from their own, half-covert, "fairness issue," the conviction that women, blacks, and Hispanics are receiving more than their "fair share," measured by the standard of equality of opportunity. Affirmative action objectifies the resentment of traditional Democrats who feel they have been shouldered aside by the party and ignored by its policies.[26]

On the whole, Democrats of this persuasion are not defending old-style racism or sexism. The many southern whites who voted for Carter in 1976 and 1980, defecting to Reagan in 1984, have adjusted to a considerable measure of formal equality, as their votes for Carter attest. And while Jerry Falwell may call on women to return to their status as "weaker vessels," Ronald Reagan suggests that a woman soon will, on her "merits," win a place on the Republican ticket. Walter Mondale recognized the strength of this resentment against the felt inequalities of opportunity. He emphasized his own commitment to "opening doors," and he suggested that American success at the Olympics was due to policies promoting racial and sexual equality. It was, however, too little and too late for 1984.

Democrats (Humphrey and Mondale) were elected, even though Mondale was defeated in 1980.

In any case, the Democrats cannot possibly abandon affirmative action. If they hope to conciliate traditional Democrats, they will have to seek new and better remedies. And the Democrats may need new sensitivities even more than a new agenda.

John Kennedy's nomination helped reaffirm the bond between Catholics and Democrats, which dates from the nomination of Al Smith in 1928, and a Catholic at the head of the ticket would certainly help to reconcile defecting Catholic voters to the Democratic Party. Yet it seems unlikely that so simple a solution will be enough. In 1960, making allowance for Protestant fears and hostilities, Catholic leaders did not object when Kennedy declared that, in public life, he would follow his conscience rather than his church. In 1984, Geraldine Ferraro took a position more conservative than Kennedy's only to become embroiled in a long, lacerating argument with Archbishop John O'Connor and other members of the hierarchy over the question of abortion.

In 1960, of course, abortion was not an issue in national politics.* It is more important, however, that changes within the church—and in the place of the church in American society—have unsettled many of the old anchors of American Catholicism. Public anti-Catholicism has virtually disappeared.† Catholic leaders, on the other hand, have become more anxious and more assertive about the orthodoxy of the flock. At the same time, lay Catholics have developed a new touchiness about their identity as Catholics because commitment to the church has become problematic and personal.‡ Catholics, more likely

---

* It surfaced first in 1972, because of McGovern's support for "free choice," and it became inescapable given the Supreme Court's decision in 1973 that abortion during the first trimester of pregnancy involves private rights protected by the Constitution (*Roe* v. *Wade*, 410 U.S. 113, 1973).

† The Protestant right grumbles, from time to time, but for the moment it is content with a kind of ecumenism that concentrates fire on the main "secular humanist" enemy. Ribuffo, *The Old Christian Right*, 267–68.

‡ For example, see the long debate on the "End of Catholicism,"

to disregard the church's teachings in private life, are also protective about the church and inclined to resent any disrespect, in public life, for its leaders and its teachings. Walter Mondale's decision to cancel his appearance at the Al Smith dinner, for example, was probably a political error; a considerable number of Catholics surely recognized that Mondale's decision sprang, at least unconsciously, from anger at Archbishop O'Connor, and many must have suspected that Mondale—even if exhausted, as he surely was—would not have missed a dinner in honor of Golda Meir or Dr. Martin Luther King.

The effect of religiously charged issues on Catholic voting is not easy to assess. Catholic teaching argues that political decisions must be made holistically, not on the basis of discrete, absolute principles. A pro-choice position on abortion, consequently, is not a fatal liability by itself.* Ferraro's views, for example, were familiar to her socially conservative, 70 percent Catholic congressional district. In her district, Ferraro was able to balance her position on abortion by support for tuition tax credits and for an antibusing amendment designed to protect neighborhood schools.† The national platform allowed no such flexibility. It seems clear that any Democratic effort to win back Catholic voters will have to offer some concessions to Catholic values and social concerns.

The Catholic hierarchy emphasized the possibilities of such a rapprochement immediately after the election. The Bishops' Pastoral Letter on poverty and economic life presented a trenchant critique of the Reagan administration's policies and a call for a national commitment to alleviate economic misery.[27] During the campaign, the hierarchy spoke almost exclusively about

centering on Thomas Sheehan's critique of the "liberal consensus" in Catholic theology. *Commonweal* 111 (21 September 1984): 490–502.

* Only 8 percent of Catholics cited abortion as a reason for their vote in 1984. *New York Times,* 25 November 1984, E2.

† Ferraro helped make it clear that opposition to busing *need* not involve racism (although obviously it often does), since she strongly supports the integration of neighborhoods.

issues like abortion; now, Father Paul Steidl-Meier writes, "the other shoe has dropped."[28] Catholic doctrine is sympathetic to economic regulation for the same reason that it often supports social regulation: it sees the law as magisterial, necessarily and rightly involved in teaching morals and shaping character as well as controlling conduct.[29] The hierarchy's campaign role, combined with the Pastoral Letter, amounted, whether by accident or design, to a message to the Democrats: Catholic teaching cannot be opposed without cost, but if accommodated, it can also be a powerful ally. It remains to be seen if the Democrats heard, or if they will respond in the same spirit.

In 1984, after all, the Democrats sent a mixed message to white ethnic communities, their old strongholds. For some time, sparked by the self-assertion of racial minorities, ethnic consciousness has been revivified in communities of east and south European extraction.[30] Governor Mario Cuomo addressed that sensibility when he spoke of the "blood of immigrants,"and in the last two weeks of the campaign, Mondale grew eloquent when he spoke of pluralistic political community.

Yet while Democratic Party rules mandate representation of women, racial minorities, Hispanics, and young people in state delegations to the national convention, they do not call for inclusion of Poles, Greeks, Italians, or other, still relatively disadvantaged nationalities. Perhaps, in this respect, the Democrats do not suffer from recognizing too many constituencies, but too few.

In fact, the Democratic Party's rules reflect an individualistic liberalism that implicitly disdains community. In the tradition of philosophic liberalism, human beings by nature are separate bodies whose merit is measured by their work. The only natural communities are defined by biological likeness—age, sex, and race—but these communities have no *moral* status. Inequalities based simply on physical differences demand special attention and correction because they breach the wall between *nature* and *political society*. Democratic Party rules, in other words, recognize women, racial minorities, and young people in order to free them from the burden of classifications that are "suspect" because they are based on qualities that were not chosen and that do not reflect achievement.

Cultural communities differ because they are based on convention, custom, and choice. To be part of an ethnic community suggests, in the individualistic view, either that one *chose* not to pursue assimilation into the middle-class mainstream or that one *failed* in the attempt, and hence any discrimination or disadvantage is, to some degree, one's own fault. Ethnic voters do not need to spell out the philosophic principles of this argument to feel and recognize its effects.*

It is probably impractical and unnecessary for Democrats to mandate formal representation of white ethnic communities. Any Democratic appeal to such voters, however, must make clear that the party respects ethnic traditions and dignities, and is devoted to the values that, broadly speaking, characterize ethnic voters: "patriotism, a strengthening of families and neighborhoods and the work ethic."[31] Jimmy Carter's campaign in 1976 profited because it seemed to promise such devotion; Carter suffered in 1980 because he had failed to deliver. In 1984, the Democratic candidates said many of the right words, but they failed to develop the Democrats' one great advantage over the Republicans, the willingness to use public power to support their verbal commitments. For ethnic voters, who tend to be economically and socially marginal and whose communities are ordinarily embattled, it is not enough to be decent; one must at least appear to be strong.

THE SOUTH AND SOCIAL VALUES

In the white South, Democratic losses are far more serious and difficult to reverse because they have carried over to the local level, suggesting a thoroughgoing change of party identification.† Moreover, southern white defections in 1984 were com-

---

* That Hispanics, a group defined by language, are at least a partial exception to the rule almost certainly underlines the distinction between favored and disfavored groups.

† According to Curtis Gans of the Committee for the Study of the

plicated by the contemporary political problem of race. The South today is hardly an egalitarian society, but memories of Jim Crow are fading, moderate southerners are less likely to feel guilt for the past and more likely to be anxious about the future. Already worried about the increasing black presence in the Democratic Party—and especially, the Democratic parties of the South—white voters were alarmed by Jesse Jackson's demand for the abolition of runoff primaries, a policy calculated to ensure black domination of state Democratic politics. Voters who would have been ashamed of the simpler forms of racism found it easy to rationalize hostility to Jackson. To white voters, Jackson suggests an inner-city hustler with an aura of financial sleaziness, self-promoting and injudicious, while Jackson's ventures into foreign policy were at least leftist and arguably unpatriotic.

It did not help that the extreme sensitivity with which Democratic leaders approached Jackson was coupled with an almost brutal disregard for the white South. Mondale selected Bert Lance to be national chairman and then abandoned him, under fire, a disloyalty made worse by the fact that the revolt against Lance centered on his connection to Jimmy Carter, not on his alleged financial peculations. To a great many voters, it must have seemed clear that Lance was subjected to public humiliation because of his connection to the South. The 1984 Democratic convention was apparently all too eager to ignore southern whites and to repudiate their leaders.*

Across the nation, evangelical religion deepened the revolt against the Democrats, but it was felt in the South with particular force. The members of the theologically conservative churches

---

American Electorate, the Republicans "are going to be a competitive party in the South, and may be the dominant party in the next six years." *New York Times*, 11 November 1984, 53. For the long-term trend in this direction, see Bruce Campbell, "Patterns of Change in the Partisan Loyalties of Native Southerners, 1955–72," *Journal of Politics* 39 (1977): 730–61.

* In choosing Ferraro as a running mate, of course, Mondale passed over the available southern candidates, and his choice of a woman was not well received in southern circles.

have traditionally been people of low income, likely to be and vote Democratic. But greater personal involvement in such churches tends to imply a greater commitment to the conservative emphasis on personal virtue and self-reliance and an increased likelihood that this conservatism will be expressed in political behavior.[32] Consequently, the "born-again" movement, with its tendency to heighten zeal and devotion, has been a time bomb for the Democrats, somewhat held in check by Jimmy Carter's very visible Christianity.* In 1984, evangelical Christians, North and South, were less likely than any other religious communion to express concern for the fairness of Reagan's policies and the most likely to cite abortion as a reason for their vote.

It is also no accident that the religious right is so deeply associated with television. Television has increased national awareness of moral and social change. It has made any number of traditionally religious people more cognizant of their embattled status, so that the claims of the religious right to speak for a "Moral Majority" amount to desperate morale building. It is part of Ronald Reagan's appeal, as *Commonweal* observed, that he understands this "sense of grievance" among the religious, the feeling of disadvantage in relation to secular culture. Reagan's apocryphal anecdotes about "court decisions" banning voluntary school prayer speak to the fear that religion is losing its place in American public life, and the president seems to offer religious Americans a chance to reclaim their "fair share" in the nation's civil religion.[33]

Even with all these disadvantages, however, the Democrats' position in the white South is not hopeless. Jimmy Carter's relative success in the South, even in 1980, suggests that recognition of the region—especially when combined with responsiveness to its religiosity—can go a long way toward holding enough white voters to tip the balance. The new Republican strength, moreover, is unstable to say the least; the GOP made similar gains in the election of 1980, only to see them disappear in 1982.[34]

---

* As Leo Ribuffo observes, however, Carter "barely qualified as an evangelical." *The Old Christian Right*, 262–63.

The old Democratic coalition is not quite Humpty Dumpty. Any chance of reassembling it, however, presumes that the Democrats can understand and respond to the "social issue," that touchstone of discontent among erstwhile Democrats. More and more Americans are aware of and disturbed by the growing fragmentation and disorder of American social life, our increasing tendency to privatism and our escalating indifference. They recognize, even if inarticulately, that social institutions—especially the family and the school—are not simply a "private" sphere separate from politics but the foundations of political life, the places where citizens are first and fundamentally educated and shaped. The health of society is necessarily the concern of any democratic regime.

Democrats recognize this, perhaps better than Republicans. They have been willing to help families, especially among the disadvantaged, and they have been deeply concerned about the growth of crimes against children. In 1984, the Democratic candidates invoked and campaigned on the basis of "family values." Yet Democrats have also been unwilling to set a *standard* for policy. They spoke of "family values" without affirming that a social unit including two heterosexual parents is the *norm* for family life on which public policy should be based. To set such a standard does not entail cruelty to single-parent families; quite the contrary, it calls attention to the difficulties under which such parents labor, and it implies the need for special public support—stronger federal laws, for example, enforcing the payment of child support. In the same sense Democrats cannot abandon their concern for the rights of gay Americans, even though that support entails political costs, but they need not maintain that homosexuality is anything but an exception to the social rule.

Liberals have been unwilling to set such a standard, fearing its punitive potential, but the lack of regulating norms makes Democratic policies seem directionless, so much formless sentimentality. Democrats will find it impossible to address the social issue successfully unless they are willing to affirm *some* moral center for social life; the fear that we are coming to lack such a foundation is what all the fuss is about. Certainly, the Democrats must accept the fact that the troubling aspects of the social issue will not, as so many liberals have hoped, simply fade away, at least not in the near future.

Finally, the Democrats would be well advised to reconsider their commitments on the vexing issue of abortion. In a sense, the abortion issue is similar to Prohibition, which split the Democrats into "wets" and "drys," except that the argument over abortion concerns first principles, the very definition of human life, and the argument is correspondingly more serious. The moral rights and wrongs aside, it is arguable that the "great experiment" in national abortion policy has failed, as Prohibition did, because it involves unacceptable political costs. Even the relatively small number of voters who cite abortion as a reason for their vote can hold the balance in a national election, and the figures overlook those voters for whom abortion is not decisive but contributes to their final choice. Americans appear to be divided into three almost equal camps: Only 29 percent would ban all abortions, but only 35 percent are in favor of "free choice"; the rest would permit abortion only in specified cases.[35] Roughly 60 percent of Americans, in these terms, regard abortion as at best an exception to the rule; support for unqualified "free choice" not only costs the Democrats strategic support, it aligns them against a conditional majority.

Of course, the Democratic Party cannot endorse any constitutional amendment that would ban abortions. It may be possible, however, to explore alternatives. Abortion could, for example, be returned to state jurisdiction, or the Democrats could accept the principle that abortion should be permitted only in some defined set of cases.[36] In any case, the Democrats will need to do some hard thinking about the principles that should govern social life.

Over the years, social conservatives have imagined, foolishly, that self-seeking and unrestrained liberty in economic life will not carry over into public life and moral conduct. They are wrong. We commit ourselves to communities, to people, or to the future only to the extent that we are confident of our knowledge of what is and will be. Instability and change make our knowledge of one another more superficial and the future more unpredictable. Since the free market implies an economy open to unregulated change, it weakens our commitments and promotes social decay.[37]

The liberal left, on the other hand, has been devoted to the decencies of sympathy and generosity, but liberals have also defended a permissive private morality, confident that it would end repression but leave compassion intact. Confronted by so many new cruelties and the insouciant selfishness reflected in Reaganism, liberalism ought to recognize its own complicity: A doctrine that defends self-expression and self-gratification lays the foundations of selfishness and self-interest and may even point to enormities. George Orwell spoke to the point:

> For two hundred years we have sawed and sawed and sawed at the branch we were sitting on. And in the end ... our efforts were rewarded and down we came. But unfortunately, there had been a little mistake. The thing at the bottom was not a bed of roses after all, it was a cesspool full of barbed wire.[38]

Even amid Reagan's jerry-built recovery, Americans are rightly worried about the moral foundations of the country. Walter Mondale did the Democrats good service for the future by championing decency. It remains to be seen if the Democrats—and, especially, the party's liberals—can learn that decency is an exacting creed, premised on self-denial. Caring for others presumes that we make their need prevail over our desire, and even a modest civility requires that private feeling yield to public form.

After 1984

The nation's moral and political future certainly lies with its youth. Today's younger voters lack a sense of their ability to change the world. Their relative conservatism, as Bernice Buresh writes, is "personal, not political," rooted in their sense of vulnerability, their desire to be reassured against the threats of a world that seems too much out of control.[39]

It makes matters worse that young Americans feel the weight of their elders so heavily. Social Security, of course, is increasingly costly, but it matters even more that older Americans clog the routes to employment, opportunity, and power. Increasingly healthy, older Americans want to work longer and, on the whole, have been able to make good their claims. Buttressed by seniority clauses and tenure provisions, older Americans are relatively protected against unemployment and economic insecurity; of workers laid off between 1979 and 1984, 40 percent were under thirty-five.[40]

White youth, in fact, has its special reasons for resenting affirmative action: Since the Supreme Court has held that seniority clauses do outweigh the claims of women and minorities, the burden of racial and sexual equality falls almost entirely on the young.[41] Senator Hart's hints that he might consider limiting increases in Social Security did not hurt him with younger voters, and Democratic charges that Reagan cannot be trusted to protect Social Security entitlements may, in this respect, have helped the president. Social Security and collective bargaining, those pillars of the New Deal, are no great assets for the Democrats among the young.

At the same time, however, younger voters have no real commitment to the GOP. They seem fond of Reagan, but it is a soft sentiment, not a strong devotion; Hart's neoliberalism attracted young voters, many of whom voted for Reagan in November, at one point giving Hart a lead over the president in the polls. Younger voters are decisively *not* ideological conservatives. They voted for Reagan on pragmatic grounds, giving him credit for strong leadership and for the recovery, but they rarely cited traditional values or conservatism as reasons for their choice. Roger Stone, a Reagan strategist, worries that too close an identification with social conservatism and the religious right may shake the fragile bond between the Republicans and the young.[42]

Shaped by change and uncertainty, younger Americans are inclined to be self-protective and fearful of deep commitments. Loyalty—especially loyalty to institutions—does not rank high on their list of virtues and disciplines. A generation shaped by television, they are more likely to judge on the basis of images and styles; as in Johnny Carson's version of Hart's campaign, "Vote for me, I have Kennedy hair," the young are more likely to be guided by the shifting externalities of appearance than the inward bonds of soul.

Democrats can hope to recover lost ground among the young, and that possibility inspires much of the Democrats' recent concern for toning up the party's image, with its vulgar fixation on Tip O'Neill's weight and rumpled appearance and its neglect of his legislative craft. Within limits, however, there is room and reason for Democrats to think about new images and new ideas. There is a conflict, however, between wooing traditional Democrats, who tend toward social conservatism, and pursuing younger voters who do not. The problem is not insuperable—Democrats have coped with a radically diverse coalition in the past—but it is a challenge to political art. The Democrats will need, in Theodore White's phrase, "to make new friends without losing old ones."[43] That exacting task demands new ideas and more; in 1988 and beyond, the Democrats will need to combine statesmanship and party government.

Some directions offer obvious possibilities. Work is the great theme uniting any prospective Democratic majority, and while there are tensions between old and young, whites and minorities, men and women, a policy of full employment aims to keep those conflicts within civil bounds by guaranteeing decent jobs for all Americans. In our society, as the New Dealers knew, employment is a virtual prerequisite of social dignity. As Robert

Kuttner remarks, "American liberals went off the track when they opted for income transfers rather than full employment as the centerpiece of their economic strategy. Means-test income transfers are very destructive. You create a separate welfare class, which is encouraged to become dependent." * The Democrats may very well want to phase down welfare in favor of some forms of "workfare," through public service employment—as in proposals for a national Police Corps or a revived Conservation Corps—or through programs—such as wage subsidies, following the Swedish example—that stimulate employment in the private sector.

There are also good reasons for the Democrats to continue Walter Mondale's late campaign theme, developing programs that support community. For some time, social disintegration has sparked somewhat sporadic efforts to preserve or create community.† By the 1980s, almost half the country, according to Daniel Yankelovich, at least *claimed* to be deeply involved in the quest for community.‡ The Democrats have at least a chance to become the champions of community, and theory as well as practice may encourage them to make the attempt. Small, reasonably autonomous, and stable communities and neighborhoods are still our best schools of citizenship, and we all pay a cost for their decline.[44]

In general, the Democrats will need to reclaim their old position as the party of those who are outsiders in the labyrinths of bureaucracy. Wherever possible, the Democrats should embrace simplification and decentralization, but they can and should argue that to dismantle the federal government would

---

* Kuttner is quoted from James Cook, "Ends and Means," *Forbes* 134 (17 December 1984): 140; see Kuttner's own *The Economic Illusion* (Boston: Houghton Mifflin, 1984).

† For example, see Harry C. Boyte, *The Backyard Revolution: Understanding the New Citizen Movement* (Philadelphia: Temple University Press, 1980), on the neighborhoods movement.

‡ Daniel Yankelovich, *New Rules: Searching for Fulfillment in a World Turned Upside Down* (New York: Random House, 1981), 251; the exact figure is 47 percent, up from 32 percent in 1973.

only leave citizens at the mercy of private power. With good reason, voters want to simplify the *process* of government, but that does not necessarily mean that they want *weak* government. Quite the contrary, it may mean that they want a government that has discretion. There is considerable evidence that the suspicions of the 1970s are waning. The Reagan administration demonstrates, rather paradoxically, that Americans want a government that at least appears strong, direct, and decisive; and in 1984, state referenda suggest that the "tax revolt" is ebbing. It may be that the electorate wants a government that is checked, not by denying it power, but by holding it accountable before the law and in political life.

The election of 1984 symbolized the beginning of the politics of the electronic age. The coming political era has its bright possibilities, but it is full of dangers as alarming as those of Orwell's imagining. Citizenship and statecraft will be more necessary than ever, but they will have to rest on new foundations. Ronald Reagan has presided over the demolition of the old politics; in the years after 1984, it will be necessary for Americans to see if they can build anew.

Notes

1. *New York Times,* 4 November 1984, E5.

2. Hedrick Smith, "Political Memo," *New York Times,* 7 December 1984, B18.

3. Alexis de Tocqueville, *Democracy in America* (New York: Schocken, 1961), 1:33, 364.

4. *The Public Papers and Addresses of Franklin D. Roosevelt* (New York: Random House, 1983), 2:11.

5. Dennis Hale and Marc Landy, "Are Critical Elections Extinct?" *Boston College Biweekly* 5 (15 November 1984): 8.

6. Tom Wicker, "The Other Fritz," *New York Times,* 3 February 1984, A29.

7. Hale and Landy, "Are Critical Elections Extinct?"

8. Tom Wicker, "After 1984, What?" *New York Times,* 23 November 1984, A35.

9. Theodore J. Lowi, *The End of Liberalism* (New York: Norton, 1969).

10. For example, see Paul F. Lazarsfeld et al., *The People's Choice* (New York: Columbia University Press, 1944).

11. *New York Times*, 8 November 1984, A19.

12. James Reston, "Insiders and Outsiders," *New York Times*, 19 August 1984, E19.

13. Walter Robinson, "Accessibility and Excessibility," *Boston Globe*, 14 October 1984, A17ff; James Reston, "Reagan Beats the Press," *New York Times*, 4 November 1984, E25.

14. David Burnham, "Experts Fear Computers' Use Imperils Government History," *New York Times*, 16 August 1984, 1ff.

15. William V. Shannon, "The Actor Comes Out in the President," *Easton Express*, 8 June 1984, A4; see the similar criticism in the *Wall Street Journal*, 16 February 1984, 62.

16. Richard Reeves, "The Ideological Election," *New York Times Magazine*, 19 February 1984, 26ff.

17. *New York Times*, 11 November 1984, 30.

18. Ashby Bladen, "The Acid Test," *Forbes* 134 (17 December 1984): 245; *New York Times*, 2 February 1984, B9, and 5 February 1984, 1ff.

19. William Serrin, "White Men Discover It's a Shrinking Market," *New York Times*, 9 December 1984, E2.

20. "New Ideas," *New York Times*, 11 November 1984, E20.

21. Gerald M. Pomper, "The Decline of the Party in American Elections," *Political Science Quarterly* 92 (1977): 21–41.

22. *New York Times*, 25 November 1984, E2.

23. *New York Times*, 8 November 1984, A19.

24. *New York Times*, 18 December 1984, B14.

25. David Rosenbaum, "Blacks in Poll Prefer Mondale to Jackson as Nominee," *New York Times*, 10 July 1984, 1ff.

26. Terry Eastland and William J. Bennett, *Counting by Race: Equality from the Founding Fathers to Bakke and Weber* (New York: Basic Books, 1979).

27. Leonard Silk, "The Bishops' Letter and U.S. Goals," *New York Times*, 14 November 1984, D2.

28. Paul Steidl-Meier, "A Reformist Document," *Commonweal* 111 (30 November 1984): 650.

29. J. Brian Benestad, *The Pursuit of a Just Social Order* (Washington, D.C.: Ethics and Public Policy Center, 1982).

30. Theodore White, "New Powers, New Politics," *New York Times Magazine*, 5 February 1984, 32, 34; Michael Novak, *The Rise of the Unmeltable Ethnics* (New York: Macmillan, 1971).

31. William V. Shannon, "Liberalism, Old and New," *New York Times*, 2 October 1976, 25.

32. Benton Johnson, "Ascetic Protestantism and Political Preference," *Public Opinion Quarterly* 26 (1962): 35–46.

33. "Mr. Reagan's Civil Religion," 484; William G. McLoughlin, "Faith," *American Quarterly* 35 (1983): 101–15.

34. Adam Clymer, "Contradictory Lessons of the 1982 Election" *New York Times*, 4 November 1982, 1, 24.

35. *New York Times*, 11 November 1984, 30.

36. David Carlin, "The Abortion Debate: Rules for Liberals," *Commonweal* 111 (21 September 1984): 486–87.

37. Daniel Bell, *The Cultural Contradictions of Capitalism* (New York: Basic Books, 1976).

38. Sonia Orwell and Ian Angus, eds., *The Collected Essays, Journalism, and Letters of George Orwell* (New York: Harcourt, Brace, 1968), 2:15.

39. Bernice Buresh, "Students, Conservative, Fearful," *New York Times*, 4 November 1984, E25.

40. Serrin, "White Men Discover It's a Shrinking Market."

41. *Firefighters v. Stotts*, 104 S.Ct. 2576 (1984).

42. *New York Times*, 25 November 1984, E2.

43. White, "New Powers, New Politics"; 34.

44. Sidney Verba and Norman Nie, *Participation in America* (New York: Harper & Row, 1972), 49.

5

Enchantment's Ending:
The Election of 1988

Yet some men say in many parts of England that King Arthur is not dead ... but rather I will say: here in this world he changed his life.

— Morte d'Arthur

A quarter of a century ago, John F. Kennedy was assassinated, and the American Camelot began to evanesce into the mists of a political Avalon. Three years earlier, in 1960, Michael Dukakis had been caught up in the enchantment of Kennedy's New Frontier; in 1988, he sought to call it back. He failed. The time for Camelot has passed, even for a candidate with more magic than Michael Dukakis possessed.

In 1988, the Democrats came back to the "Boston-Austin ticket" that had succeeded in 1960—a Massachusetts liberal with ethnic credentials paired with a moderate Texan. Electoral logic now works against a northeasterner at the head of such a ticket, however; in 1988, Democrats suspected (with reason) that they could have won with Bentsen as their presidential nominee. In 1960, the combination of Lyndon Johnson and traditional party loyalty was strong enough to enable Kennedy to carry most of the South. In 1988, Bentsen's presence on the ticket was insufficient to win even one southern state.

Race and economics have reduced Democrats to a minority of southern whites, an unreliable constituency, sufficient to win in coalition with black voters, but one that requires special cultivation.[1] Locally, biracial coalitions are frequent and often decisive in the South, as they were in 1986; but no Democratic presidential nominee other than Jimmy Carter has assembled such a majority since the federal protection of voting rights transformed southern politics. For Democrats, this trend is probably crucial: southern votes were essential to three out of their four postwar presidential victories, and in the fourth, LBJ's 1964 landslide, Democrats carried all but the Deep South.[2]

These days, moreover, the Democrats have no support to spare; Michael Dukakis did a good job of bringing Democrats home, only to discover that this was not enough. Conservatives outnumber liberals; Dukakis did not approach Kennedy's appeal to Roman Catholics; the political weight of the cities and industrial states, "the last Democratic trench"—is in decline.[3] Even the good news for the Democrats in 1988, their gains in the Midwest and West and their ability to stall or roll back Republican gains among the young, only emphasized the decreased importance of the Northeast and the party's heritage. In 1987, Robert Shrum gave the Democrats good, if unheeded, advice: "The Democratic Party has lived off the legacy of John F. Kennedy for twenty-eight years. The torch will go out unless it finally passes to a new generation. We need to invent a new legacy."[4] The "Kennedy business" did not help Dukakis, A.M. Rosenthal wrote at the end of the campaign, because "the young do not vote for the dead."[5]

And yet, Rosenthal is right only in a very narrow sense. Yesterday's events shape today's allegiances, language frames thought, and dead kings and citizens do live on, shadowy, in the body politic.[6]

A century ago, in *A Connecticut Yankee in King Arthur's Court*, Mark Twain described another effort to update Camelot. Sent back in time, Hank Morgan, the Connecticut Yankee, tries to bring Arthur's Britain into the nineteenth century through a combination of technological mastery and showmanship. In 1988, each of the Yankee candidates—no one was deceived by Bush's pose as a Texan—had his technical credentials—Bush's

Washington experience set against Dukakis's managerial miracles—but neither was much for flair. Bush, guided by his media "handlers," did better than his rival (although Hank Morgan would probably have called Bush's posturings the "magic of folde-rol"), and inevitably, many Democrats incline toward the argument that Dukakis's defects as a campaigner cost them the election.

It may be so. But in Twain's story, for all his gifts as a performer, Hank Morgan fails to transform Britain. The Connecticut Yankee relies on technology and material progress to produce a republic; but the church, the Yankee's nemesis, keeps control of birth, marriage, and death, the events that punctuate the life of the human spirit. Hank Morgan's politics fail because he neglected the soul. His catastrophe can serve as a cautionary tale.* The election of 1988 sent an urgent signal that something is wrong with the political soul of American democracy.

Public Life and Private Media

The campaign was more than "negative." It was a year when civility "took it on the chin," one in which, on talk shows as in politics, nastiness "became a commodity."[7] Even so, it had precedents.

In 1888, President Grover Cleveland, who had survived considerable tarring four years earlier, faced smears and distortions at least the equal of 1988.† His former opponent, James G. Blaine, charged that Cleveland had appointed to office 137 convicted criminals, including 2 murderers, 7 forgers, and several brothel keepers. Mrs. Cleveland was forced to deny the rumor that the president beat and abused her. It was said that

---

* Doubly so, since the proximate cause of disaster in Twain's story is a stockmarket crunch engineered by Sir Lancelot.

† R.W. Apple recalled Cleveland's experience in relation to the Hart fiasco (*New York Times,* 8 May 1987, 1ff), and Charles Paul Freund invoked it in comparison to the campaign (*Washington Post National Weekly,* 7–13 November 1988, 29–30).

Cleveland was a dogmatic liberal (of the nineteenth-century variety) and the equivalent of a "secular humanist" because he was reported to have said "I believe in Free Trade as I believe in the Protestant religion."

Most notoriously, Matt Quay, the Republican boss of Pennsylvania, engineered a scheme by which a Republican supporter, posing as a former British subject, wrote to the British ministry, asking which candidate would best advance Britain's interest. The minister, Lionel Sackville-West, injudiciously replied that Cleveland's free trade sympathies made him preferable, and Republicans exultantly portrayed Cleveland as unpatriotic and, especially in Irish wards, as the tool of British imperialism.[8]

Nevertheless, there is something new and alarming about the incivilities of the presidential campaign in 1988. In the first place, the electronic media give greater force and currency to scurrilities, just as television makes innuendo visible: Blaine's attack on Cleveland's appointments had nothing like the impact of a glowering Willie Horton, illustrating Republican claims that Dukakis had been "soft on crime," or of pictures of garbage afloat in Boston harbor. Moreover, contemporary voters are more exposed to and dependent on mass media.

In Cleveland's day, the press could still be described, in the terms Tocqueville used earlier, as a form of political association. There was a mass press, but the great majority of newspapers were local, the voices and guardians of community. Information from national campaigns and leaders reached most voters only through local editors, leaders, and opinion makers who interpreted it and passed on its propriety and authenticity.[9] In 1988, the media spoke to more and more citizens directly, without intermediaries; gatekeepers could not protect us when the fences had been trampled or pulled down.

In 1888, American politics was still dense with associations, and for both parties, the presidential candidate was only the chief figure in a campaign made up of a myriad of local campaigns in states and wards. Cleveland, in fact, did not campaign at all, considering huckstering beneath the dignity of his office, and Benjamin Harrison's more active office-seeking was very limited by our standards.[10]

Law and technology have combined to create a centralized presidential politics dominated by national media and party committees. In campaigns, as in voting, congressional and local elections are sharply distinct from the presidential contest, so much so that it seemed anomalous, on election night, when candidates for governor and U.S. senator in Montana received about the same percentage of the vote as their party's nominee for president.[11]

The "nationalization of the electorate" has been a major political theme of the century, the result of an effort to "open" politics to individual citizens, freeing them from the control of local elites. Progressive reformers, advocates of the primary system, were also inclined to celebrate the mass media, just as their successors urged "a more responsible two-party system."[12] In one respect, the breaking down of racial barriers to political participation, the process has been pure gain. It has become increasingly clear, however, that the grand design of the reform tradition has failed.

Despite prolonged campaigning, despite vast expenditures of money (in which, in 1988, the two parties were virtually equal), despite the advice of experts and the easing of rules for voter registration, turnout fell—as it has, with the exception of the New Deal years, throughout this century. This "demobilization" of the electorate is too profound and too persistent to be explained by the requirement of registration or other barriers to voting.[13] In 1988, the fraction of adult Americans who went to the polls was almost 20 percent lower than it was in 1960, when racial discrimination still kept masses of black Americans off the electoral rolls. In Todd Gitlin's axiom, "As politics grows more professional, voting declines." * The affective distance between citizens and public life is great and growing. When they

---

* Todd Gitlin, "The Candidate Factory," *Boston Review* 13 (August 1988): 6. Implicitly, critics acknowledged the point when they faulted Dukakis's campaign for being "too thin"—too centralized and

vote for president, voters must evaluate candidates whose characters they know only superficially, for an office in which character is crucial.* We lack the "peer review" that, in earlier
years, was provided by party leaders and opinion makers who
controlled nominations and guided campaigns. In 1884, the discovery that Grover Cleveland apparently had fathered an illegit-
imate child provoked the response that such private failings,
then as now the focus of media attention, are not the most important indices of *political* character, and Cleveland won the
election.† In 1988, by contrast, while Gary Hart's derelictions
shattered his candidacy, voters did not appear to notice that, after all his years in the Senate, Hart was endorsed by only one incumbent Democratic senator. Judgment by peers is yielding to
an "audition" by the media, and private proprieties may now
outweigh public virtues.‡

Be that as it may, citizens *are* dependent on mass media for
news and for the interpretation needed to make sense out of the
bewildering ravelments of contemporary life.[14] At the same
time, the media are great concentrations of power, remote and
distant "private governments" that decide who will speak to us
and on what terms.[15] In the media's version of deliberation, citi-

---

too little inclined to reach out to local party leaders—and overreliant on
"experts." See *New York Times,* 12 November 1988, 8; and Michael
Barone, "Those Dukakis Ads Just Don't Work," *Washington Post National Weekly,* 17–23 October 1988, 29.

  * James David Barber, "How to Pick Our Presidents," *New York
Times,* 8 March 1987, E23, observed that within broad limits, "the man
makes the office."

  † Since James G. Blaine, Cleveland's opponent, combined private
rectitude with public sleaziness, Moorfield Storey argued that "we
should elect Mr. Cleveland to the public office he is so admirably qualified to fill, and relegate Mr. Blaine to the private life he is so eminently
fitted to adorn." Mark DeWolfe Howe, *Portrait of an Independent* (Boston: Houghton Mifflin, 1932), 151.

  ‡ Michael Arlen, "The Candidates Deserve Each Other," *New
York Times,* 28 September 1988, A27; it is doubtful that JFK—and possibly even Franklin Roosevelt or Dwight Eisenhower—would have met
the media's moral test for the presidency.

zens have no voices; one cannot "talk back" to a television set, and citizens can assert their dignity only by refusing to listen.* Of course, a displeased viewer can also change channels, but this "receiver control" is almost entirely negative, given the media's tendency toward a homogenized message.[16]

Yet media decision makers know that, while the power of the media as a whole is overawing, any *single* medium is vulnerable, its position still more precarious because media domination invites resentment. Changing channels is as easy as it is because national television has no organic relation to our lives; a local newspaper or radio station is part of, and often indispensable to, the day-to-day life of a community, but there is no reason why I should prefer ABC to NBC or CBS. The older media, especially the local press, had a position that permitted them to offer "cue giving"—guidance as well as protection—and evaluation was an integral part of their reporting. The electronic media are more anxious to "resonate"; more fearful of giving offense, they cultivate nonpartisanship and a professional neutrality.[17]

Better than the Democrats, the Republicans have understood that this desperate neutrality makes it easy to neutralize the media. Fairly consistently, Republican candidates criticize the media, appealing to the public's fear of "hidden persuaders" and joining its resentment of media power. George Bush virtually began his campaign with a contrived faceoff with Dan Rather, and he continued to fault the media's coverage of the election. This "media bashing" takes the form of asking for fair play or "balanced" treatment, but its real aim is to insulate a candidate—or a president—from criticism, Teflon-coating its beneficiaries.

The success of this strategy was evident in the media response to this year's presidential and vice-presidential debates. After the first debate, the media pronounced the exchange a

---

* Richard Sennett, *The Fall of Public Man* (New York: Knopf, 1977), 283. Of course, many Americans do talk back to the television set—my father-in-law was particularly eloquent—in a response that is probably healthy but certainly futile.

draw, a defensible stance even if a plurality of viewers thought Dukakis had edged Bush. Even John Chancellor's astonishing claim that Dan Quayle had done well, despite Lloyd Bentsen's one-sided victory, might be explained as a too-rigid refusal to take sides. But television newsmen showed no reluctance to declare that Bush had won the second presidential debate. Taken as a whole, these comments suggest that if the media did not approach Republican candidates "on bended knee"—Mark Hertsgaard's description of the Reagan years—they did bend over backward.[18]

Even at its best, however, television reporting (and increasingly, all reporting) shies away from evaluating the substance, or even the accuracy, of what is said in campaigns, preferring to discuss the strategy and process of campaigning.[19] Nominally neutral, this emphasis on stratagems effectively tells citizens that the *public* side of politics—and, especially, those questions being argued—is of secondary importance. Even pure quantities, like results of polls and elections, need to be interpreted in the light of "momentum" and "expectations." In this implicit teaching, "real politics" is covert, "a business for professionals" that can be approached only through "inside" information supplied by the media.[20]

Parties and candidates, of course, struggle to control the process of interpretation, bypassing the press whenever possible and controlling "photo opportunities" through carefully contrived events. In 1988, for example, the Dukakis campaign, after beginning with relatively frequent press conferences, followed the Republicans' example in shielding the candidate from the press.[21] Similarly, both national conventions were transparently staged to avoid any appearance of conflict and to project optimism, harmony, and concern for "family values." Ironically, the 1988 conference of the Communist Party of the Soviet Union featured heated debate, resembling an old-style American party convention as much as the 1988 American conventions called to mind the traditional, totalitarian gatherings of the Communist Party.[22]

"Packaging," however, only redefines the role of the media; by pushing debate and decision offstage, it makes citizens even more dependent on the media to search what is said in public for clues to the real deliberations behind the scenes. Public life, increasingly, is mirroring the media's art; portrayed as trivial or superficial, political events become lifeless and shallow, arguments for cynicism and indifference.[23]

Inherently, the electronic media emphasize the private, self-protective, and individualistic side of American culture at the expense of citizenship and public life. Traditional politics, like older forms of entertainment, drew citizens into public places; the media bring politics to individuals in private retreats. In those settings, private concerns are naturally uppermost, making it harder than usual—and it is always difficult—to appeal to public goods and goals.[24] Politics is dramaturgical: it asks us to step beyond the day-to-day, to see the present in the light of the possible, judging practice by theory. Great politics, like great theater, requires a special space, a precinct for its particular sort of fantasy, from which we reemerge into everyday life. Such distinctions hone and heighten experience; by blurring fantasy and reality so pervasively, television weakens reality's force and fantasy's charm.[25]

Above all else, television is a visual medium, confined to what can be seen and hence to externalities. Sight is our quickest sense, but it is also superficial, and the media's discontinuity of image and affect encourages emotional detachment, adaptation rather than commitment. A politics of the visible comes naturally to, and teaches us to be, a "world of strangers."[26]

At the most fundamental level, politics is about invisible things. A political society can be symbolized—for example, by the flag, George Bush's talisman in 1988—but it cannot be *seen*. Especially in a polity as diverse as the United States, political community is not a matter of outward semblance but of inward likeness, common ideas and ideals. In this sense, television almost necessarily distorts politics, since it is forced to visualize and personalize things that are impalpable or objective.[27] When events suit the medium, as in television's coverage of the southern civil rights movement, it speaks with unique power, but more often it is apt to be misleading, silly (Dukakis's tank ride), or mischievous.

To classical political theory, speech, not sight, is the most political of the faculties because it is in and through speech that we discover the boundaries and terms of political community.[28] But political speech—and, especially, *listening* to political speech —is a skill and pleasure that must be learned; it demands an extended span of attention, the capacity for critical reflection, and that art of hearing that lets us separate meaning from its disguises. Always difficult, that command of rhetoric is harder to cultivate in a society as supersonic as ours, and the electronic media actually undermine the arts of speech and hearing.*

Preoccupied with holding their audience, television programmers shun anything that might bore us (the Republican argument, this year, against more than two presidential debates), a logic that tends toward the lowest common public denominator.[29] The 1988 debates were question-and-answer sessions in which no comment could run longer than two minutes; in 1960, Kennedy and Nixon began their debates with eight-minute opening statements. In the 1970s, the average "sound bite" allowed a public figure was 15 to 20 seconds, and the president was given as much as a minute. Pretty thin at best. But in the 1980s, the figure has declined to 10 seconds for *all* public figures.† It symbolizes the decline of speech that George Bush, admiring the refrain, made "Don't Worry, Be Happy" into a campaign song, either ignoring the words or trusting that American voters would not notice their very contrary lesson.[30]

---

* Marc Landy and I made a similar argument in "On Political Edification, Eloquence and Memory," *PS* 17 (1984): 203–10.

† Gitlin, "The Candidate Factory," 7. Hoping to encourage more substantive discussion, Michael Woo, a Democratic member of the Los Angeles City Council, sensibly suggested legislation requiring political ads on television to be purchased in longer blocks of time. *New York Times,* 13 November 1988, E3.

"Almost the only pleasure of which an American has any idea," Alexis de Tocqueville wrote, "is to take part in government and to discuss the part he has taken," and even women "listen to political harangues after their household labors."[31] More recently, Frank Skeffington, Edwin O'Connor's fictional mayor, spoke of politics as America's "greatest spectator sport," in which performers could, at least, rely on a critical mass of knowledgeable fans, but Skeffington was already sounding "the last hurrah."[32] In 1988, public speech seemed to be degenerating into shouted incivility, the tough talk of playground squabbles, at best a preface to politics.

The Parties and the Nominations

The primaries worked, in a sense, although the nominating process was too long, too costly, and too much influenced by unrepresentative electorates. The cost in time and dignity helped keep out some of the most attractive Democratic possibilities, but the primaries sorted out a number of flawed candidates, and the eventual nominees were sensible and able. The electorate, however, did not like the choice, with some reason. Democratic Party discontent has a special point, since the primary system puts the party at a strategic disadvantage in presidential politics.

Contested primaries, the rule for Democrats, are associated with defeat in presidential elections. In the last quarter-century, the only Democratic victories occurred in 1964 and 1976, when Republicans had their own bitter internal struggles.[33]

In any election, candidates of the center have a tactical advantage, since they have the best chance of making themselves "acceptable" to a broad coalition. In primary elections, this edge is not always decisive: Candidates "win" primaries by coming in first, and they do not need majorities. In 1988, Dukakis received 42 percent of all Democratic votes cast in primaries, but until the Pennsylvania primary he was under a third, and his victory in Texas, crucial to his eventual nomination, was won with just less than 33 percent of the vote. The primary victor, consequently, can be, like Goldwater or McGovern, the candidate of party militants, who are more likely to participate in primaries. In a contest for the nomination, a centrist is usually the best a party can hope for.

Nevertheless, a candidate who stands in the center of his or her party will be considerably to the right or left of center in relation to national opinion. Primaries pull candidates away from the national center, especially since primaries deemphasize economic issues, about which parties agree, and emphasize intraparty disagreements on foreign policy and social issues, the rallying points of party militancy.[34] Michael Dukakis is a centrist Democrat and no hero to liberals in his own state, but, as George Bush happily observed, Dukakis was forced by the logic of the primaries (especially in Iowa and New Hampshire) to stress his liberal credentials, his membership in the ACLU, and his devotion to peace. These sincere convictions, identifying Dukakis as substantially left of center, indicated his vulnerability. Before his contests with Jackson and rise in the polls induced temporary blindness, it was clear that Dukakis, unable to stir voters anywhere, was too liberal to win even moderate conservatives. Dukakis, James Reston wrote, would "lose the South and bore the North," and so it proved.[35]

For Republicans, it was a near thing: a shift of 7300 votes in New Hampshire would have made Senator Dole the victor in that state, at least lengthening the contest and, given Dole's gift for vituperation, raising the possibility of a donnybrook. As it was, the Republicans avoided a prolonged primary campaign, and they wound up with a candidate at least moderate and possibly better described as part of the party's liberal wing. Beginning with the nominee closer to the center of national opinion, the Republicans enjoyed an advantage that could be countered only by a superior Democratic campaign.

That campaign, of course, did not materialize, for which the primaries also bear some limited responsibility. The effort to capture a nomination establishes habits that persist, in the candidate and his or her staff, in the campaign proper. Part of Dukakis's primary success derived from his refusal to be drawn into intraparty conflict; his reliance on vague, liberal, but relatively unprogrammatic appeals; and his rejection of negative campaigning. Part temperament, part calculation, Dukakis's tactics within the party foreshadowed his failure in the national campaign.*

The problem posed by the primaries is bad news for Democrats, since their party is much less cohesive than the GOP. Republicans declare themselves the party of individual liberty and opportunity, which translates broadly into a defense of property and profit; the Democrats' standard is "equal justice," a much harder term to define. Democrats require deliberation and tests of strength to work out the terms and frame of party coalitions.

There is some balm for Democrats in the offing. Blessed with an incumbent president, the Republicans will probably be able to avoid a primary battle in 1992, though even that is no sure thing. "Main Street" Republicans—the ideological right, buttressed by the party's growing evangelical wing—are almost certain to be frustrated and enraged by the "Wall Street" cast of the Bush administration. That partisan fault line, already rumbling, seems likely to shake Republican foundations, in 1996 if not sooner.[36]

Democrats cannot afford to be much comforted. For the immediate future, Democrats must expect primaries shaped by the candidacy of Jesse Jackson, based on Jackson's support among blacks and the white, middle-class left, the "Peugeot proletariat."[37] Jackson's vote is remarkably stable—from Super Tuesday to the end of the primary campaign, Jackson's percentage of the Democratic vote rose only from 26 to 29—but numbers are not the whole story. Jackson inspires negative coali-

---

* Dukakis and his staff may have mistaken for positive support what was only antipathy to Jackson, especially since the voters who rejected Jackson as "too liberal" would obviously be vulnerable to later Republican appeals. Scot Lehigh, "Michael Dukakis: The Unmaking of a President," *Phoenix's The NewPaper,* 10 November 1988, 4; *New York Times,* 27 April 1988, A24.

THE POLITICS OF DISAPPOINTMENT

tions; race injures him with many voters, and by most, he is perceived as too radical, possibly anti-Semitic, and certainly unelectable. Consequently, unless another candidate can dent Jackson's support in either of his two constituencies, the primary campaign is likely to be defined by the effort to establish which candidate is the alternative to Jackson. And that goal, obviously, will exaggerate the already disproportionate influence of the early primaries.*

It makes matters worse for the Democrats that money plays so decisive a role in primary campaigns. In general, Democratic money comes from liberal donors, which accentuates the pressure on candidates to establish their ideological bona fides. Since the material interests of liberals often run counter to their political commitments, they have no reason to value an electoral success that is not a victory for principle. Republicans also have their ideologues, of course, but in general, Republican donors see an economic interest in victory that moderates their zeal for pure doctrine. Nevertheless, even Republicans know the problem: The primaries displace those who live "off" politics in favor of those who live "for" politics, which imposes a strain on the political center.†

In what has become a quadrennial ritual, the Democrats will tinker with the nominating process. (In fact, they began to do so at the 1988 convention where Dukakis made important concessions to Jesse Jackson.) But the primaries are almost certainly too well established to permit a return to a nomination controlled by professionals, and more modest reforms have so

---

* Since Jackson's nomination was not a real possibility, his candidacy meant—and probably will mean—that black voters have only a negative influence on the Democratic nominee. Juan Williams, "How Jackson Is Jeopardizing the Influence of Blacks," *Washington Post National Weekly,* 15 June 1987, 23.

† The distinction derives from Max Weber, "Politics as a Vocation," in *From Max Weber: Essays in Sociology,* ed. Hans Gerth and C. Wright Mills (New York: Oxford University Press, 1946), 77–128; on the contemporary aspects, see Thomas Byrne Edsall, *The New Politics of Inequality* (New York: Norton, 1984).

far proved ineffective.[38] For example, "superdelegates," introduced to strengthen the role of professional judgment, have been pretty much irrelevant. Largely elected officials, they are bound to be leery of opposing any candidate who leads after the primaries, even if they think him a loser. In a democracy, it is never safe to resist the "people's choice," and the interest of superdelegates in doing so is lessened by the fact that their own chances of election seem so independent of the national ticket. There is something to be said for Robert Beckel's suggestion that 60 percent of the delegates be chosen by primaries and the rest by state parties, but that proposal almost certainly offends too many interests to be adopted.

Democrats can and may do something to establish a national campaign staff, independent of the retinues of candidates, which can make plans for a campaign against the Republicans while the primary season is still going on. Such a planning staff might lessen an important Republican advantage: it might attract senior Democrats, who are disinclined to commit their time and prestige to the uncertainties of a primary campaign.[39] Even the shrewdest and best designed reforms, however, will only better the ability of Democrats to cope with their inherent disadvantage in the nominating process and the difficulty it implies for the campaign.

Politics and Memory

In one important sense, the Democrats, as the "out party," began the campaign one-up on the Republicans. The party in power must defend the whole of its record; the opposition can choose the aspects of that record on which to base its challenge. The "outs" can promise to continue the popular aspects of the administration's program while correcting its flaws; if the "ins" pledge to do likewise, they will be asked why they have failed to act before. Discontent and the desire for change were the foundations of Dukakis's early lead and shaped his strategy of limiting criticism of Reagan and his policies in favor of the "upbeat" theme, "The best America is yet to come."[40]

But the choice between change and the status quo is never the whole story. The appeal to political memory may allow the party in power to present a different choice: not what *they* promise as opposed to what *we* have done, but what *they* did as contrasted with what *we* have done. Fear or resentment of the past wars with hope for the future in our judgment of the present.[41]

Until recently, memory was a Democratic fortress, recalling the Great Depression and World War II, the glory years of the Roosevelt era—and in the South, where memories faded more slowly than in the North, nursing the straight-ticket heritage of Reconstruction. Now those old remembrances are quieting into whispers, losing their connection to contemporary partisanship, especially since, wounded by change and the media, our political memory is growing shorter.[42] Even the Kennedy years, so important to Dukakis, were only a flickering of the Democrats' candle of memory, obscured by the dark years that followed.

Increasingly, the focus of American political retrospection is Vietnam and the turbulence of the 1960s, permissive morality, stagflation, and the decline of America's imperium, the "greening of America" turned overripe. Out of that half-remembered experience, conservatives—but preeminently Ronald Reagan —have shaped a new, mythic history epitomized by the "L word," liberalism identified with the Carter years, but also with all the excesses of the late 1960s and the 1970s.[43] Ironically, Republicans also benefit from the New Left's critique, which, by portraying liberals as hypocritical and lukewarm, helped build the image of liberalism as morally soft. It is part of Reagan's art, moreover, that implicitly he ran against Nixon as well as Carter, appealing to the distaste for government reinforced by Watergate, assimilating Nixon's era to the "night" dispelled by Reagan's "morning." Where Democrats once ran against Hoover, Republicans ran against McGovern in 1988, and George Bush argued repeatedly that "neighborhood Democrats" should prefer him to a leadership dominated by "the remnant of the '60s."[44]

Up to a point, Democrats recognized the problem and sought to correct it. Dukakis emphasized work rather than welfare and party leaders insisted on a shortened platform, unburdened by many controversial planks. The Democratic convention featured the author and folk-hero Garrison Keillor, surrounded by children; and Jimmy Carter, praising past Democratic candidates, asked, "Wouldn't Ed Muskie have made a wonderful President?" Symbolically, Carter was reversing the verdict of 1972, attempting to write George McGovern out of Democratic history. In the same spirit, Michael Dukakis, despite his supposed disregard for symbols, was careful, early in the campaign, to invoke Harry Truman and to make a pilgrimage to Lyndon Johnson's birthplace, and it was Truman's liberalism with which he identified himself toward the end of the contest.

Yet to overcome the Republican version of the past, Dukakis needed a vision of the future, a language of the common good. He never articulated one, and the lack was more noticeable because the appeal to "community" in his acceptance speech was the rhetorical high point of the campaign.[45] More was involved than Dukakis's too-apparent shortcomings as an orator. He betrayed an uneasiness with the idea of community in both the infrequency and artificiality of his references to his ethnicity (despite its obvious political potential) and his choice to respond legalistically to slurs on his patriotism.[46]

It cost him. After the convention, Dukakis's severest losses were among Catholics, a decline most visibly linked to his views on crime, but most fundamentally to the emphasis, in Catholic teaching, on the idea of political society as a moral order.[47] The second presidential debate, his last real chance, was a disaster. Asked what his reaction would be were his wife raped and murdered, he responded with an abstract—and rehearsed—statement of his views on crime; portraying himself as one to make "tough choices," he declined to say what taxes he would raise should it become necessary, refusing to deal with the possibility, even as a hypothesis.[48] Dukakis was unwilling or unable to find words that, validating personal experience, would subordinate it to citizenship, bridging the distance between private feeling and the public good. But that is what his campaign required.

Michael Dukakis came of age in the 1950s, the Silent Decade, when politically interested students were preoccupied with totalitarianism and McCarthyite repression, and intellectuals elevated the "separation between facts and values" into a dogma, convinced—wrongly—that it leads logically to tolerance.[49] Ideology was "unmasked" to reveal its roots in the interests of groups and classes, and social scientists discerned its impending end.[50] Politics, in these terms, could be reduced to "brokerage," the arrangement of compromise between groups, perfected by able management and skilled administration.

Political science helped make "interest-group liberalism" into "the new public philosophy."[51] A political generation learned to cultivate "realism," a pragmatic "tough-mindedness" that scorns sentiment in favor of "hard fact." That teaching lies behind Michael Dukakis's extraordinary assertion that the issue between him and George Bush was "competence"; it was also the weakest side of the Kennedy years, the illusion of "the best and the brightest."[52]

For all his faults, however, John Kennedy retained a certain Irishness: he set his pragmatism to a poetry that sent hopes dancing. Yet Kennedy was surely no ideologue; suspect on civil liberty and no enthusiast for civil rights, he often seemed to the right of Nixon on issues of foreign policy. In this sense, George Bush's charge was appropriate: Michael Dukakis is a liberal, at least when compared with his hero, and the campaign in 1988 could not be a replay of 1960.

In one critical respect, however, George Bush is more akin to Michael Dukakis than either is to the great presidents. Bush gave little indication of any idea of public purpose beyond an individualist's devotion to the private sector, the "thousand points of light." His hope for a "kinder and gentler America," consequently, seems to amount to no more than a promise to administer and broker private initiatives so as to moderate conflict. Bush, wrote George Will in disgust, "skitters like a waterbug on the surface of things," and James Skillen observed that both Bush and Dukakis are fundamentally "managerial coordinators," who use language to "buy time" rather than articulate an idea of the common good.[53] The candidates in 1988 reflected the fears and hesitancies of the contemporary public mind, but not the ability to lead or elevate it, and in the end, they confirmed the electorate's disenchantment.

Liberalism, Politics, and Economics

Republican success in attacking the "L word" obscured the fact that political liberalism, more broadly defined, was a worldbeater in 1988. Modern liberalism grew up as the advocate of the Positive State, exemplified by the New Deal, urging the use of government, "the common instrument of political democracy," to meet human needs and take on problems that, as individuals, we are too weak to address.[54] In 1988, regulation and intervention were climbing back into favor, and active government commanded broad support.[55]

The Republican platform did not advocate the elimination of a single government program, and George Bush plumped for day care and youth employment. Nevertheless, economic policy was basically a Democratic talking point, and Michael Dukakis scored when he talked about such economic programs as nationwide health insurance. The Republicans gained the whip hand, however, because they were more willing to extend the positive state into foreign policy—Dukakis was hurt by his questions about the Grenada invasion and by a fear that he would endanger "peace through strength"—and into social life.

Bush moved ahead by advocating public support for "values" in civic education, most visibly in his zeal for the Pledge of Allegiance and his defense of school prayer.[56] His stance on abortion also helped, although his waffling entailed some embarrassing moments. Having expressed sympathy for a "Right to Life" amendment, Bush upheld abortion in cases of rape and incest, or to protect the life of the mother, and once he had "sorted out" his views, advocated criminal penalties only for the doctors performing illegal abortions, not for the women who obtain them. Yet even this moderate—or muddled—persuasion favored more government intervention than Dukakis's position in favor of a woman's "right to choose." Bush rejected abortion on demand, as Dukakis did not, and Bush's vacillations put him squarely in the center of American opinion.*

Most important, Bush succeeded in portraying himself as the champion of stronger law enforcement, chiefly by arguing for the death penalty for "cop killers" and "drug kingpins." This deprived the Democrats of what had looked to be a major asset. The Democrats began with an unwonted claim on the social issue because the administration looked weak on drugs: "Just Say No" failed to make use of state power, and the government seemed compromised and craven in its dealings with Panama's Noriega. Dukakis, however, offered no distinctive antidrug program, and his views on the death penalty, together with Willie Horton's infamous furlough, helped establish the image of Dukakis as a militant civil libertarian and soft on crime.

---

* On George Bush's early statement of his views, see Robert Zwier, "George Bush," *Public Justice Report* 11 (January 1988): 4. On 1 December 1987, the *New York Times* reported that an identical percentage of Republicans and Democrats (37 percent) favored the existing system of abortion rights, while 40 percent of Republicans *and* 43 percent of Democrats favored limiting abortion to cases of rape, incest, and protecting the life of the mother (p. B24). Abortion divides both parties, but it is more polarizing to Democrats who, on both sides of the issue, appear to feel more strongly than Republicans. See Lewis Bolce, "Abortion and Presidential Elections," *Presidential Studies Quarterly* 18 (1988): 815–27. Of course, Bush's position is an administrative nightmare: Would a woman be entitled to an abortion merely by claiming rape or incest? If she is required to substantiate the charge, what would the standard of proof be? And could a decision be reached within the first trimester, or even the period of gestation?

In this, as in so many things, it seemed a bad year to oppose big government and public power.

That conclusion, however, is one-dimensional. Our culture has always been divided between the individualism of philosophic liberalism and the communitarian strain most powerfully expressed by biblical religion.[57] It is not surprising, consequently, that Americans look to government for more services but also regard it suspiciously and support it grudgingly, demanding tough laws but distrusting public authority, recognizing their own vulnerability but clinging to private liberty.

Modern America magnifies the reasons for skepticism. Government and politics are baffling and frustrating, especially at the national level. To enter public life is to be convinced of one's unimportance; political life forces a confrontation with indignity, even when it hints that the "arts of association" may hold the key to another sort of honor. Private life, by contrast, affords an illusion of control, especially in relatively prosperous times.

John Kennedy's grace helped give a charm to politics, but Kennedy's assassination (and the assassinations of Dr. King, Malcolm X, and Robert Kennedy), together with disillusioning experience, emphasized dangers and limitations, weakening the personal attractions and moral claims of public life. Dan Quayle, as Lloyd Bentsen observed, is no Jack Kennedy; today, the rich and the would-be rich, the bright and the handsome, are apt to gravitate toward private pursuits. Shrunk to the measure of the yuppie, Kennedy's image is caricatured by Donald Trump and Alex Keaton.

So much of government's recent record, after all, seems to tell against it. Lyndon Johnson, so forceful and adroit, overreached in Vietnam and overpromised in the War on Poverty. Nixon, despite his reputation as a Machiavelli, stumbled into Watergate; and Carter, who profited from mistrust of government, proved a marplot, additionally cursed with bad luck. For a time, the public thought Ronald Reagan had "taken charge," but the Iran-*contra* affair revealed him to be feckless, ill informed, and indecisive, a virtual figurehead whose best defense was that he did not remember, or had never known, what was going on. Reagan retained his popularity, but the electorate, forced to recognize his shortcomings, received another jolt to its confidence in government and its judgment of political leaders.

Paradoxically, Reagan's pratfall may have helped George Bush. Bush was a safe candidate, a known quantity. Many voters felt that Michael Dukakis might be a great president, but prodded by the Republican campaign and Dukakis's own missteps, they came to fear that he might be terrible. Given the recent record of failed presidencies, most such voters preferred not to take the chance. Dukakis's vagueness only made matters worse, since it left voters without a clear sense of what he would do.

Moreover, Dukakis's appeal to his "competence," like Bush's own managerialism, may have fed the suspicion that democratic politics, including the presidency, no longer controls the nation's destiny. In the first place, we know that American life is more and more affected by events and decisions in foreign countries over which the U.S. government has only a measure of influence. We bluster, but we are becoming accustomed to the limits of American power.

Second, in the sphere that does remain to government, bureaucracy plays an often esoteric but increasingly central role. Authority has everywhere a tendency to pass downward, "into the body of the organization."[58] The Executive Office burgeoned in order to help the president control the executive branch; now the agencies of the Executive Office enjoy a sometimes startling independence from presidential control. For years, political scientists have warned that the president is in danger of being made a captive of his own machinery, and while the best modern presidents have fought that tendency, the drift is there.[59]

Harry Truman insisted that "the buck stops here" precisely because he understood, following *The Federalist*, that the price of presidential authority—and, especially, of the "inherent power" of the prerogative—is a willingness to be held accountable for mischances and the misdeeds of others.[60] The diffusion of power, however, makes it seem more and more inappropriate to think of the president in terms of rule and unfair to hold him strictly responsible for execution. By contrast, it is now common to refer to the president as a manager, a coordinator of policies initiated and carried out elsewhere.

When John Kennedy accepted responsibility for the Bay of Pigs, he meant that it was his decision and that he held himself accountable for the plan, its execution, and its failure. When Ronald Reagan declared himself "responsible" for the Iran-*contra* imbroglio (and before that, for the bombing of the Marine barracks in Beirut), he meant that he was *legally* accountable, but he went to some lengths to disclaim *personal* responsibility, and his language—"Mistakes were made"— directed the blame to a subjectless organizational process. Reagan's preposterous innocence made it easier for him to make such arguments; Lyndon Johnson could never have persuaded us that he did not know the details of the Iran-*contra* policy. Nevertheless, Reagan indicates the direction of things: accountability is shrinking into a thin political fiction.

Kurt Vonnegut saw it more than thirty-five years ago, imagining a future America in which government had become separate from politics and hence from civic deliberation and direction. In Vonnegut's fantasy, the president was a former actor —"he had gone directly from a three-hour television program to the White House"—and his job amounted to a kind of media show:

> All the gorgeous dummy had to do was read whatever was handed to him on state occasions: to be suitably awed and reverent, as he said, for all the ordinary, stupid people who'd elected him to office, to run wisdom from somewhere else through that resonant voicebox and between those even, pearly choppers. . . . Just as religion and government had been split into disparate entities centuries before, now, thanks to the machines, politics and government lived side by side, but touched almost nowhere.[61]

The doubt that politics makes, or can make, more than a trivial difference to our lives calls into question the possibility of self-governance and hence the basis of the American republic. This evidently concerns all parties and all citizens, but it should be particularly disquieting to Democrats, since theirs is preeminently the party of the state, the champion of "citizenship values against market values." *

Democrats need to remind themselves, moreover, that this "civic ethic" holds, in principle, that economic interests are subordinate and do not deserve to rule, in the country, in the self, or in the party. For Democrats, this is not an entirely comfortable teaching. Divided between the culturally most modern and most traditional groups in America, Democrats would prefer to avoid "social issues" and broader questions of value; scarred by Bush, the Dukakis campaign hoped to "drive such questions off the political, agenda and replace them with economic concerns." † In general, most voters did see the Democrats as the defenders of their interests, and Dukakis's late campaign—"I'm on your side"—drew most Democrats home. It was not enough. Economic concerns will blot out everything else only when economic problems are overwhelming, as they were in the Great Depression. They could not do so amid the relative prosperity of 1988.

In any case, economic interests are clearly inseparable from questions of foreign policy, just as social concerns are linked to economic phenomena like the two-wage-earner family. In fact, the need to shore up our economic culture—pride in work, commercial rectitude, and willingness to save—is probably the most important economic issue confronting the republic.[62]

The "American Century" is ending in a mood of dread; Americans worry about the country's future even when they are

---

* Robert Kuttner, *The Life of the Party: Democratic Prospects in 1988 and Beyond* (New York: Viking, 1987), 15; in what follows, I am indebted to Kuttner, *Life of the Party*, 205–47.

† E.J. Dionne, "Political Memo," *New York Times*, 29 September 1988, A1. On Democratic divisions, see Bolce, "Abortion and Presidential Elections."

more or less confident about their personal fortunes. Conservative cheerfulness seemed forced—"Be Happy," the Bush theme song, is eerily parallel to the depression favorite, "Ain't We Got Fun"—and a great many Americans voted for Bush not so much because they believed he could avert the day of reckoning but because they expected him to postpone it.[63]

Debt towers. In eight years, America has changed from the largest creditor to the largest debtor nation, and public and private borrowing has become an economic way of life. To alarm Americans with memories of the Carter years, George Bush did not refer to the magnitude of inflation; he recalled the sky-high interest rates of Carter's last year, imposed in the (successful?) attempt to drive inflation down. Implicitly, Bush realized that Americans do not mind paying dearly if they can borrow cheaply, but the public is never quite able to forget that we are discounting the future to pay for the present.

Americans are also uneasily aware of the trade deficit and the apparent decline of American products in the international economy. They see foreigners buying U.S. assets and suspect it is "on the cheap."[64] Long accustomed to something like economic autarky, Americans are still uncomfortable with our increasing dependence on foreign economic decisions, even though our new vulnerability is subtler and easier to ignore than the oil shortages of the 1970s.[65] And as Paul Kennedy argues, political power tends to follow the path of economic decline.[66] Pridefully, Americans used to quote Berkeley's vision of America's future, "Westward, the course of empire takes its way." No more: American preeminence seems to be passing, like that of the ancient empires, moving farther west across the Pacific.*

About their personal economic prospects, Americans are mostly optimistic, but there are reasons for disquiet. Poverty, although increasing, is still distant from most, but they are disturbed by homelessness, its most visible form.[67]

---

* George Berkeley, "On the Prospect of Planting Arts and Learning in America" (1752). Berkeley would be as disturbed as most Americans, since he prophesied that America's rise would "close the drama."

More and more Americans sense—and many know by experience—that upward mobility, the opportunity celebrated by Republicans, is becoming difficult, and even a middle-class standard of living is harder to attain. Jobs are less secure, and the preponderant evidence indicates that the new jobs being created are not "good jobs at good wages." From 1980 to 1986, average personal wages fell 2 percent (discounting inflation), and household incomes rose 10 percent only because of women entering the workforce, a resource now substantially spent.

Americans have long been accustomed to achieving a middle-class standard through borrowing, a strategy made even more necessary by the fact that college costs are rising faster than families' ability to pay. Young Americans, however, are likely to find this burden heavier, and perhaps unsupportable, because future gains in prosperity are likely to fall short of expectations. Over the succeeding decade, the wages of a thirty-year-old worker in 1950 increased 58 percent, and in 1960, 44 percent; by 1977, the figure had fallen to 21 percent.[68] "It is a true rule," John Winthrop argued, "that particular estates cannot subsist in the ruin of the public."[69] He was right: Our personal economic destinies cannot be separated from the country's shadowed future. The private centers of power in American postindustrialization are a source of problems rather than solutions. Americans are unsettled by mergers, "junk bonds," and "leveraged buyouts," and they are troubled by corporate power generally. In a *Washington Post* poll, 66 percent of Republican voters (as opposed to 14 percent of GOP convention delegates) agreed that corporations have "too much power."[70]

In 1932, Berle and Means described the separation of ownership from control, the growing ascendancy of managers over stockholders in the modern corporation.* Today, however, managers seem unable to protect themselves against takeovers, even with such innovations as the "poison pill" defense. Finance, always powerful, has become imperial, and it sometimes seems

---

* A.A. Berle and Gardiner C. Means, *The Modern Corporation and Private Property* (New York: Macmillan, 1934).

that managerial bureaucracy, displacing politics in public life, is *being* displaced in economic life.* On Wall Street, observers note a radically short-term orientation in which wealth and control have become separated from production. At the center of our economic life, a contemporary version of "conspicuous consumption" is undermining the discipline of productivity.[71]

Liberalism, Values, and Community

Yet, discontent with this "conservative permissiveness" in the economy is only part of the broader feeling that society is out of control, falling toward Gehenna. Every day's news—if not everyday experience—testifies to the frequency of disordered families, child abuse, child neglect, and teenage suicide. And for millions of voters in 1988, the drug problem ranked first among political issues.[72]

The difficulty is more fundamental than such tumults; it can be heard even in the silences of contemporary life. American households are radically mobile—somewhere around 20 percent of Americans move every year—and we learn to be fearful of attaching ourselves to people or places in order to avoid the pain that comes with uprooting. Divorce, now commonplace, underlines that lesson, and even stable families are more and more apt to be limited to two generations (only about 25 percent of American children have a significant relationship with a grandparent), a setting that teaches Americans that important relationships are short term.

Illustratively, in a 1988 television ad, a young girl, separated from her friends by her family's move, complains that she does not make friends easily. A motherly employee of the mov-

---

* The vulnerability of managers is not much comfort to ordinary stockholders, although corporate raiders sometimes present themselves as allies of investors, as Gordon Gekko did in the movie *Wall Street*. Even when stockholders make profits, "golden parachutes" (payments to displaced managers) and "greenmail" (payments by management to raiders) indicate the shareholders' basic disadvantage.

ing company reassures her, "You've already made one. Me."
Yet, obviously, this slight acquaintance with an adult who, because of her job, will also soon be moving on, is no substitute
for the intimate ties the girl has lost. The ad offers only the cool
counsel that such transient relationships may be the best we can
hope for, and, as at least one news story reminds us, closer
bonds may not be safe. In Wisconsin, two teenage friends, unable to bear the separation when one family moved away, ended
a weekend reunion in suicide.[73] Experience cautions Americans
to keep their relationships shallow, their liabilities limited, and
their obligations minimal.

Shouting that individuals are insignificant, contemporary
America also whispers the more seductive lesson that, in consequence, they are free from responsibility and that it is not even
legitimate to hold them accountable. Lewis Lapham describes
that temptation:

> A man can feel shame before an audience of his peers, within
> the narrow precincts of a neighborhood, profession, army
> unit, social set, city room, congregation, or football team. The
> scale and dynamism of American democracy grants the cease-
> lessly renewable option of moving one's conscience into a
> more congenial street.[74]

And it is predictable, if unedifying, that the dominant
moral doctrine of the media is a version of relativism and the
ethic of success.[75]

Despite all that, Jimmy Carter was right to discern a
"moral hunger" in the electorate, a yearning attested by the remarkable success of Allan Bloom's *The Closing of the American
Mind,* with its appeal to natural right and to the enduring clas-
sics of Greek antiquity.[76] Yet America is too diverse and Americans are too accustomed to the benefits of modern commercial
society to admit of a return of traditional morality and community, especially since Americans have enough memory of Jim
Crow to know that community can be repressive. The past that

holds the broadest appeal in popular culture is recent, though stabler: *Who Framed Roger Rabbit?* is likely to be contemporary America's closest approach to the trial of Socrates.*

At the same time, civil order—and, especially, a democratic one—does require and rest on shared beliefs and principles.[77] In regimes that are not democratic, the culture of the ruling elite can be the foundation for political life; democracy presumes a much broader sharing of civic ethics and culture. Democratic debate is possible only about matters we are willing to submit to the judgment of majorities, and so presumes that we are minimally confident in the public's decency and idea of justice. It is the things not in debate that make democratic argument possible, as Tocqueville observed in an earlier America:

> Thus, in the moral world, everything is classed, adapted, decided and foreseen; in the political world, everything is agitated, uncertain and disputed: in the one is a passive, though voluntary, obedience; in the other an independence, scornful of experience and jealous of authority. These two tendencies, apparently so discrepant, are far from conflicting; they advance together, and mutually support each other.[78]

Tocqueville worried, however, that individualism, embedded in the laws, would eventually eat up those public and private virtues he called "the habits of the heart," and there is evidence that just such an imbalance is developing in American culture. Robert Bellah and his associates found that Americans are losing the languages of biblical religion and civic republicanism, the historic rivals of individualism in our national dialogue. Even when Americans act in terms of these older values, they tend to explain and justify their lives in the language of utilitari-

---

* Frederic Jameson, "On Raymond Chandler," *Southern Review* 6 (1970): 624–50. In Vonnegut's *Player Piano*, workers displaced by technology do not long for a world without machines, but one in which they are needed to tend and repair machines.

anism, calculated self-interest, or "expressive individualism," the appeal to private feeling.[79] Too many "modern people" have "sadly concluded" that "greed is the universal motive, sincerity is a pose, honesty is for chumps, altruism is selfishness with a neurotic twist and morality is for kids and saints and fools."[80] At the same time, like Glaucon in Plato's *Republic,* they long to be persuaded that it isn't so.[81]

A great deal of Ronald Reagan's abiding popularity reflects his effective appeal to patriotism and "traditional values," but this rhetoric, while important, must be set against a record of symbols and policies that forward individualism.[82] Neither Ronald Reagan nor George Bush has been willing to ask Americans for sacrifice, and where their policies have imposed burdens, they have almost universally fallen on the less fortunate.

In foreign affairs, the Reagan administration celebrated cheap victories, but it shied away from policies that involve significant costs. Verbally firm on terrorism, the Reagan administration hesitated to risk the lives of hostages, pursuing its secret negotiations with Iran. Despite the importance of Nicaragua in Reagan's worldview, he preferred covert action to either an open use of prerogative or an all-out, popularity-risking effort to persuade the public.[83] And conservatism's social issues, with their challenge to contemporary middle-class lifestyles, were never high on Reagan's political agenda and probably rank even lower for George Bush.[84]

In part, this reticence derives from the accurate calculation that Americans are unwilling to make more than modest sacrifices. At bottom, however, Republicans are individualists in principle, devoted to the private sector and to private gain. In the second debate, George Bush assailed Michael Dukakis's plans to make tax evaders pay, saying that they would lead to "IRS agents in your kitchen." (Characteristically, Dukakis let slip the chance to call his opponent soft on law enforcement.) On the other hand, Democrats have failed to make clear that they understand that political community is more than "inclusiveness," that it imposes duties as well as rights.

This was the deeper dimension of the argument over the death penalty and law enforcement that hurt Dukakis in 1988. At the Democratic convention, Dukakis's invocation of community spoke, as his citation of John Winthrop indicated, to the biblical elements of the American tradition and to all the resonances in our culture that are older than the individualism of liberal philosophy. Political community, however, presumes, as a ruling principle, some idea of the common—and, ultimately, of the human—good. Communitarianism sees political society as a moral order, and the laws of such a regime, designed to strengthen what is admirable and right, entail penalties for the wicked as well as rewards for the virtuous.*

By contrast, philosophic liberalism begins with autonomous individuals, and it rejects the idea of a single human good. Political society, in this view, has no moral mission, no goal to shape the soul. It exists to advance private rights more effectively, and public policy is properly a calculation of utilities.† Liberalism is always hesitant to punish because it doubts that, strictly speaking, there is any wrong: there are only rights carried to excess, as in the saying "We have a right to do as we please, so long as it does not infringe the rights of others." Obviously, liberals can and do punish, but they are more comfortable with the effort to cure the "underlying conditions" of crime by providing positive incentives to civil behavior.‡

To ask whether the death penalty "deters," as Dukakis did, is to range oneself on the liberal side of the debate, seeing punishment in terms of utilities and from the criminal's point of view. It also misses the vital communitarian point that decent

---

* For what follows, I am indebted to Stanley C. Brubaker, "Can Liberals Punish?" *American Political Science Review* 82 (1988): 821–36; see also Michael Sandel, *Liberalism and the Limits of Justice* (Cambridge, England: Cambridge University Press, 1982), 89–91.

† Thomas Pangle, *The Spirit of Modern Republicanism* (Chicago: University of Chicago Press, 1988); for a modern example, although one that nominally rejects individualism, see David Truman, *The Governmental Process* (New York: Knopf, 1951), 50–51.

‡ Such incentives evidently work in the long term, if at all.

citizens are not "deterred" primarily by the likelihood of punishment—if that were the case, America would be in even worse straits—but by the idea that crime is wrong.[85]

In a troubled society, citizens look to government to vindicate their decencies and to protect public life from simply private-spirited calculation. Periodically, any political society must call on its citizens to risk their lives, to suffer economic loss, and to disrupt their relationships on behalf of the public good. Citizenship, like civility, begins with a form of self-denial, a willingness to see oneself as a part of a whole. Punishment balances the scale, imposing on vice a homage to civic virtue, and a political society that is too gentle with crime or avarice will find, in the not so very long run, that it has lost its citizens.*

Toward Public Renewal

Abler and less hollow than his predecessor, George Bush may be willing to grapple with the nation's deeper problems.† Republicans have no immediate interest in tampering with their formula for success in presidential elections (although as memories fade, it will grow harder to run against the late 1960s and the Carter era.)[86] By contrast, Democrats have every reason, at least as a presidential party, to attempt to articulate a view of the common good.[87]

In the first place, Democrats need a more positive, less

---

* "In a good state," Rousseau wrote, "there are few punishments, not because pardons are frequent but because criminals are few.... When pardons are plentiful, it is a sure sign that crimes will soon have no need of them, and everyone can see where that leads." Jean-Jacques Rousseau, *Social Contract,* bk. 2, chap. 5.

† *Bush had his moments, not only in foreign policy, but also in recanting his foolish pledge never to raise taxes (even though, under pressure from the right, Bush later apologized for this departure from ideological orthodoxy). As most Americans saw, however, Bush had no particular goals for America beyond a cautious desire to keep the ship afloat.* —Author note, 1995.

apologetic foreign policy.[88] This is a matter for delicacy, since Democrats are far more divided than Republicans in their attitudes toward international affairs; in a 1987 poll, Democrats divided almost equally when asked whether the United States should "support anticommunist forces around the world."[89] Even that polarization, however, argues against dovishness and for moderation, and there is a special urgency to the need for a new Democratic perspective on foreign policy.

There are unmistakable signs that the "Vietnam syndrome" is ending. Even more dramatically than the Vietnam memorial, Jane Fonda's apology to veterans signals the war's new place in national remembrance, and the rise of courses on Vietnam in nonelite colleges is a political omen Democrats cannot afford to ignore. This change is an opportunity for Democratic reconciliation, since lines are softening on both sides of the Vietnam divide. The controversy over Dan Quayle's military record established or revealed a new, lower conservative standard, by which patriotism is satisfied by law-abidingness: one did one's duty, George Bush implied, by refraining from burning draft cards or flags.

This is as clear a portent as Ronald Reagan's divorce was in social policy: conservatism is adapting, and opinion in contemporary America, while not dovish, is also not on the side of the hawks.[90] If Ronald Reagan can become an apostle of arms control, it should be possible for Democrats to lose their reflex against the use of military force, avoiding their recent tendency to overgeneralize the "lessons" of Vietnam. (Senator Bill Bradley has already set an excellent example.) Perhaps some Democrat may even observe that both those who fought in Vietnam and those who resisted the war filled a fuller measure of patriotism than those who merely obeyed the law.

In any case, Democrats surely need to offer some examples of "toughness," some instances of willingness to punish and to enforce standards of civil conduct, if they are to be credible advocates of political community. Locally, even very liberal Democrats, like Assemblyman Jack O'Connell in California, are apt to support stricter sentences, including the death penalty, and Congress was wise in voting to enforce child-support payments.[91] Beyond particular policies, Democrats have a special reason to demonstrate that their party has a vertebral moral identity. The Democratic Party cannot weaken in its advocacy of racial and gender equality; it is probably committed to a pro-choice position; and the list goes on. Committed to change in so many areas of life, Democrats must demonstrate to the electorate that, more than weathervanes, they have some principles that do not change.*

This is nowhere more evident than in relation to race, the "dirty little secret" of the election of 1988.[92] Actually, it was not much of a secret. There is more and more willingness to speak about the drift of whites away from the Democratic Party, and not only in the South. Among Democratic candidates since Franklin D. Roosevelt, only Lyndon Johnson received the support of a majority of whites, and Johnson's revolution helped persuade a large number of working-class white voters that, in the last analysis, Democrats will prefer the interests of blacks to their own.[93]

At the same time, it is harder to overcome such feelings by an appeal to guilty consciences.† Legal segregation is a hazy memory, and for the most part, overt racism has yielded to subtler forms. For example, in the media—and hence in the view of most Americans—race is visible largely in relation to crime and the sleazier forms of interest-group politics.

Philosophic liberalism offers little help. The primacy of individual rights in the liberal tradition implies that equality, "before the law" and in politics, exists to protect earned in-

---

* And only ruling principles give the party a claim on those who dissent from its social positions, particularly its stance on abortion. See David Carlin's fine "It's My Party," *Commonweal* 115 (7 October 1988): 521–22.

† *In the aftermath of 1994, the assault on affirmative action, now more aggressive and less apologetic, has even begun to attract Democratic support.* —Author note, 1995.

equalities in economic and social life. Enforced integration of low-income housing runs against property rights; busing menaces plans to give one's children the benefit of superior public schools; affirmative action seems to endanger the basic principle of equal opportunity, that jobs should be awarded on the basis of demonstrated ability. Liberal doctrine does recognize the claim of minorities to compensation for past injuries, but its individualism, rejecting the idea of collective guilt, argues that I am responsible only for my own deeds, not those of the past. Policies to promote racial equality are increasingly likely to be seen, in these terms, as "reverse discrimination," violations of the unequal prerogatives of private achievement.

Democrats cannot counter that persuasion, let alone overcome it, without a language of collective obligation. In the biblical view, for example, membership makes citizens participants of the whole of a political society's life, including its heritage. When citizens say that in 1776, "we" declared our independence from Great Britain, they identify with the American past, but this appropriate pride also entails guilt: Our Constitution included slavery, and our society perpetuated racism. "In Adam's fall," the Puritans taught their children, "we sinned ALL."

In that understanding, all Americans have an obligation to make those sacrifices that are necessary to atone. The burdens this involves should be shared as equally as possible: Working-class whites in cities like Yonkers should not be expected to welcome low-income housing when rich, neighboring cities like Scarsdale are left alone. When individual Americans suffer some loss in the interest of racial equality, however, it is no different in principle from conscription, which may call some to serve in time of war while leaving others at home. Every citizen has a civic calling to repay his or her debt to the common life.

Implicitly, by pledging "equal justice," the 1988 Democratic platform went beyond pluralistic inclusiveness. Equality makes its own discriminations. We are not equal in the way we look or in what we have achieved; since equality rejects the testimony of such appearances, it points politics toward the soul. Moreover, a politics founded on the belief in equality excludes racism and relativism, for it holds that what is human is more important than biology or culture.[94] There is also a contemporary truth in the promise of just equality, with its suggestion that equality can be unjust.

America cannot be an ancient Greek *polis* or a homogenous community; political life must find room for our diversities and our privacies, just as prudence must acknowledge the impact of technology and economic change. American democracy needs, and can stand, only so many stanzas of epic poetry; contemporary politics calls for the more prosaic effort to protect and rebuild locality, association, and party, the links between private individuals and public goods. Even such limited goals, however, presume policy guided by a ruling principle, that middle term between repression and relativism whose better name is citizenship.[95] For both Republicans and Democrats, the election of 1988 indicates the need for a new civility, and for the kinds of word and deed necessary to affirm, for the coming century, the dignity of self-government.

Notes

1. Harold W. Stanley, William T. Bianco, and Richard Niemi, "Partisanship and Group Support Over Time," *American Political Science Review* 80 (1986): 969–76; E.J. Dionne, " 'Solid South' Again, but Republican," *New York Times,* 13 November 1988, 32; John Herbers, "A Few but Sturdy Threads Tie New South to the Old," *New York Times,* 6 March 1988, E 1.

2. Paul Abramson, "Measuring the Southern Contribution to the Democratic Coalition," *American Political Science Review* 81 (1987): 569.

3. The phrase is from E.J. Dionne, "Political Memo," *New York Times,* 20 October 1988, A1.

4. *New York Times,* 12 May 1987, 16.

5. "On My Mind," *New York Times,* 4 November 1988, A35.

6. Ernst Kantorowicz, *The King's Two Bodies* (Princeton, N.J.:

Princeton University Press, 1957).

7. Lena Williams, "It Was a Year When Civility Really Took It on the Chin," *New York Times,* 18 December 1988, 1ff.

8. Matthew Josephson, *The Politicos* (New York: Harcourt, Brace, 1938), 46; Allan Nevins, *Grover Cleveland: A Study in Courage* (New York: Dodd, Mead, 1932), 428ff; and Allan Nevins, ed., *The Letters of Grover Cleveland* (Boston: Houghton Mifflin, 1933), 183–84, 188–89.

9. Alexis de Tocqueville, *Democracy in America* (New York: Schocken Books, 1961), 1:204–15; Sally Foreman Griffith, *Home Town News: William Allen White and the Emporia Gazette* (New York: Oxford University Press, 1988).

10. Josephson, *Politicos,* 423–24, 427.

11. Jeffrey R Abramson, F. Christopher Arterton, and Gary R. Orren, *The Electronic Commonwealth* (New York: Basic Books, 1988), 11–13; Joseph Schlesinger, "The New American Party System," *American Political Science Review* 79 (1985): 1152–69.

12. Laura L. Vertz, John P. Fendress, and James L. Gibson, "Nationalization of the Electorate in the United States," *American Political Science Review* 81 (1987): 961–66; William J. Crotty, *Political Reform and the American Experiment* (New York: Crowell, 1977); Committee on Political Parties of the American Political Science Association, *Toward a More Responsible Two-Party System* (New York: Rinehart, 1950).

13. *Providence Journal,* 10 November 1988, A11.

14. W. Russell Neuman, *The Paradox of Mass Politics: Knowledge and Opinion in the American Electorate* (Cambridge, Mass.: Harvard University Press, 1986).

15. Paul Corcoran, "The Limits of Democratic Theory," in *Democratic Theory and Practice,* ed. Graeme Duncan (New York: Cambridge University Press, 1983), 19; *The Nature of Politics: Selected Essays of Bertrand de Jouvenel,* ed. Dennis Hale and Marc K. Landy (New York: Schocken Books, 1987), 44–54.

16. Abramson, Arterton, and Orren, *Electronic Commonwealth,* 15, 46–49; Todd Gitlin, *Inside Prime Time* (New York: Pantheon, 1985), 325–35.

17. Abramson, Arterton, and Orren, *Electronic Commonwealth,* 13.

18. Mark Hertsgaard, *On Bended Knee: The Press and the Reagan Presidency* (New York: Farrar, Straus and Giroux, 1988).

19. Kathleen Hall Jamicson, "Is the Truth Now Irrelevant in Presidential Campaigns?" *Washington Post National Weekly,* 7–13 Novem-

ber 1988, 28.

20. Gitlin, "The Candidate Factory," *Boston Review* 13 (August 1988): 23.

21. Eleanor Randolph, "Now There Are Two 'Stealth Candidates,'" *Washington Post National Weekly,* 26 September–2 October 1988, 14.

22. James North, "While the Soviets Debated, We Poured on the Pablum," *Washington Post National Weekly,* 5–11 September 1988, 25.

23. Eugene J. Alpert, "The Media and the Message," *Political Science Teacher* 1 (Summer 1988): 13; John Chancellor, "Putting Zip, Juice—Interest—into Campaigns," *New York Times,* 29 November 1988, A25.

24. Abramson, Arterton, and Orren, *Electronic Commonwealth,* 177; Gitlin, *Inside Prime Time,* 330, 332; Daniel Boorstin, *The Americans: The Democratic Experience* (New York: Random House, 1973), 393.

25. Barbara Lippert, "Ronald Reagan and Michael Jackson—Together at Last," *Washington Post National Weekly,* 5–11 September 1988, 24; Robert Brustein, "Can Bush as Bush Steal the Show?" *New York Times,* 21 August 1988, E25.

26. Gitlin, *Inside Prime Time,* 248.

27. T.W. Adorno, "Television and the Problem of Mass Culture," in *Mass Culture,* ed. Bernard Rosenberg and David Manning White (New York: Free Press, 1957), 435.

28. Aristotle, *Politics,* 1253a, 9–18.

29. Dorothy B. James, "Television and the Syntax of Presidential Leadership," *Presidential Studies Quarterly* 18 (1988): 737–39.

30. *New York Times,* 14 October 1988, A14.

31. Tocqueville, *Democracy in America,* 1:293.

32. Edwin O'Connor, The *Last Hurrah* (Boston: Little, Brown, 1956), 70; cf. Frank Kent, *The Great Game of Politics* (New York: Doubleday Doran, 1935).

33. Martin P. Wattenberg, "The 1988 and 1960 Elections Compared: What a Difference Candidate-Centered Politics Makes," paper presented at the annual meeting of the American Political Science Association, Washington, D.C., 1–4 September 1988.

34. Byron Shafer, "Scholarship on Presidential Selection in the United States," *American Political Science Review* 82 (1988): 962.

35. *New York Times,* 4 April 1988, A21.

36. Philip Weiss, "The Cultural Contradictions of the GOP," *Harp-*

ers 276 (January 1988): 4–58. In Iowa, Robertson did better than Dole among younger voters and three times better than Bush.

37. The phrase is from Richard Morin, "Jackson's White Support Is the 'Peugeot Proletariat,' " *Washington Post National Weekly,* 2–8 May 1988, 37.

38. James Lengle, "Democratic Party Reforms: The Past as Prologue to the 1988 Campaign," *Journal of Law and Politics* 4 (1987): 233–73; David Broder and Paul Taylor, "The Democrats' Problem," *Washington Post National Weekly,* 14–20 November 1988, 12.

39. *New York Times,* 12 November 1988, 8.

40. David Broder, "For Dukakis, the Glass Is Half Full," *Washington Post National Weekly,* 2–8 May 1988, 4; and "An Uncertain Electorate Is Tilting Democratic," ibid., 4–10 July 1988, 12.

41. Morris P. Fiorina, *Retrospective Voting in American National Elections* (New Haven: Yale University Press, 1981).

42. John Garvey, "Age of Distraction," *Commonweal* 114 (25 September 1987): 40.

43. Michael Wallace, "Reagan and History," *Tikkun* 2, no. 1 (1987): 13–18; Seymour Martin Lipset, "Americans Sneer at Liberalism, Why?" *New York Times,* 28 October 1988, A35.

44. *Washington Post,* 29 October 1988, A17; Paul Taylor, "Bush Has Dukakis Trapped in a Time Warp," *Washington Post National Weekly,* 10–16 October 1988, 13.

45. Scot Lehigh, "Michael Dukakis: The Unmaking of a President," *Phoenix's The NewPaper,* 10 November 1988, 6.

46. David Broder, "What Dukakis Should Have Said," *Washington Post National Weekly,* 19–25 September 1988, 4; Edward Walsh, "An Immigrant's Kid for the Immigrants," ibid., 6–12 June 1988, 7.

47. E.J. Dionne, "Political Memo," *New York Times,* 20 October 1988, A1.

48. On the second debate, see *New York Times,* 12 November 1988, A1ff.

49. Steven D. Stark, "The Mandate in the Gray Flannel Suit," *Washington Post National Weekly,* 6–12 June 1988, 24–25; Leo Strauss, *Natural Right and History* (Chicago: University of Chicago Press, 1953), 35–80.

50. Daniel Bell, *The End of Ideology: On the Exhaustion of Political Ideas in the Fifties* (Glencoe, Ill.: Free Press, 1960).

51. Theodore J. Lowi, *The End of Liberalism: Ideology, Policy, and the Origins of Public Authority* (New York: Norton, 1969).

52. Bruce Miroff, *Pragmatic Illusions: The Presidential Politics of John F. Kennedy* (New York: McKay, 1976); Robert Gaines, "Cursing the Darkness," *Phoenix's The NewPaper,* 10 November 1988, 1ff.

53. George Will, "A National Embarrassment," *Washington Post National Weekly,* 3–9 October 1988, 33; James Skillen, *Public Justice Report* 12 (October 1988): 6.

54. Robert Kuttner, *The Life of the Party: Democratic Prospects in 1988 and Beyond* (New York: Viking, 1987), 13. The classic statement of modern American liberalism is John Dewey, *The Public and Its Problems* (New York: Holt, 1927).

55. By almost 2 to 1 (60 to 33 percent), Americans responding to a poll late in 1987 rejected any cut in government services. *New York Times,* 1 December 1987, B24.

56. Michael Robinson, "Can Values Save George Bush?" *Public Opinion* 11 (July/August 1988): 13, 59–60.

57. Michael Kammen, *People of Paradox* (New York: Knopf, 1972).

58. John Kenneth Galbraith, "Coolidge, Carter, Bush, Reagan," *New York Times,* 12 December 1988, A16.

59. Edward Corwin, *The President: Office and Powers* (New York: New York University Press, 1957), 300–304.

60. *The Federalist,* No. 70.

61. Kurt Vonnegut, *Player Piano* (New York: Dell, 1952), 118–19.

62. Amitai Etzioni, "The Party, Like Reagan's Era, Is Over," *New York Times,* 16 February 1987, 27; Michael Lerner, "Neo-Compassionism," *Tikkun* 2 (November/December 1987): 12.

63. Benjamin Friedman, *Day of Reckoning: The Consequences of American Economic Policy under Reagan* (New York: Random House, 1988); Marie Natoli, "Campaign '88," *Presidential Studies Quarterly* 18 (1988): 714.

64. John Berry, "The U.S. Trade Deficit Won't Vanish Overnight," *Washington Post National Weekly,* 11–17 January 1988, 20.

65. Jeffrey Garten, "How Bonn, Tokyo Slyly Help Bush," *New York Times,* 21 July 1988, A25.

66. Paul Kennedy, *The Rise and Fall of Great Powers* (New York: Random House, 1987); Lester Thurow, "A Briefing for the Next President," *New York Times,* 21 August 1988, F2.

67. Tom Wicker, "Always with Us," *New York Times,* 19 November 1987, 27.

68. Frank Levy, *Dollars and Dreams* (New York: Russell Sage Foundation, 1987); Paul Blustein, "The Great Jobs Debate," *Washing-*

ton *Post National Weekly,* 5–11 September 1988, 20–21.

69. "A Modell of Christian Charity," in *Puritan Political Ideas,* ed. Edmund Morgan (Indianapolis: Bobbs-Merrill, 1965), 90.

70. *Washington Post National Weekly,* 15–21 August 1988, 10.

71. James Glassman, "The Monster That's Eating Wall Street," *Washington Post National Weekly,* 18–24 January 1988, 23; Etzioni, "The Party, Like Reagan's Era."

72. The phrase "conservative permissiveness" is from Kevin Phillips, "The Reagan Revolution Is Over and the GOP Should Be Grateful," *Washington Post National Weekly,* 17 August 1987, 23. On the general point, see Daniel Goleman, "How Is America?" *New York Times,* 25 December 1988, E12; and Daniel P. Moynihan, "Half the Nation's Children Born without a Fair Chance," *New York Times,* 25 September 1988, E25.

73. *New York Times,* 18 October 1988, A29.

74. Lewis Lapham, "Supply-Side Ethics," *Harpers* 270 (May 1985): 11.

75. Herbert London, "What TV Drama Is Teaching Our Children," *New York Times,* 23 August 1987, H23ff.

76. *New York Times,* 22 November 1987, 37; Allan Bloom, *The Closing of the American Mind* (New York: Simon and Schuster, 1987).

77. Bennett Berger, "Disenchanting the Concept of Community," *Society* 25 (September/October 1988): 50–52; Michael J. Himes and Kenneth R. Himes, "The Myth of Self Interest," *Commonweal* 115 (23 September 1988): 493–98.

78. Tocqueville, *Democracy in America,* 1:33.

79. Ibid., 2:118–20; Robert Bellah et al., *Habits of the Heart* (Berkeley: University of California Press, 1985).

80. Walt Harrington, "Has Truth Gone Out of Style?" *Washington Post National Weekly,* 4–10 January 1988, 6–7.

81. Plato, *Republic,* 358D.

82. Christopher Lasch, "Traditional Values, Left, Right and Wrong," *Harpers* 273 (September 1986): 13–16.

83. Russell Baker, "Talk So Big, Do So Nothing," *New York Times,* 29 March 1986, A27.

84. Steven V. Roberts, "Reagan's Social Issues: Gone but Not Forgotten," *New York Times,* 11 September 1988, E4.

85. Brubaker, "Can Liberals Punish?" 831.

86. Robert Samuelson, "End of the Carter Era," *Newsweek,* 14 November 1988, 59.

87. Kuttner, *Life of the Party,* 210; Bruce Babbitt, "The Democrats' Long Road Back," *New York Times,* 15 November 1988, A31.

88. Mark Shields, "If the Democrats Are to Win in '88," *Washington Post National Weekly,* 11–17 January 1988, 28; A.M. Rosenthal, "On My Mind," *New York Times,* 4 November 1988, A35.

89. *New York Times,* 1 December 1987, B24.

90. E.J. Dionne, "Reopening an Old Wound," *New York Times,* 23 August 1988, A1ff; Fox Butterfield, "Disparity in College Courses on Vietnam," *New York Times,* 27 April 1988, B11.

91. Anthony Kohlenberger, "Jack O'Connell: The Grass-roots Politician," *California Journal* 19 (November 1988): 478.

92. Anthony Lewis, "The Dirty Little Secret," *New York Times,* 20 October 1988, A27.

93. Harry McPherson, "How Race Destroyed the Democrats' Coalition," *New York Times,* 28 October 1988, A31; Edward G. Carmines and James A. Stimson, *Issue Evolution: The Racial Transformation of American Politics* (Princeton, N.J.: Princeton University Press, 1988).

94. See my essay, "What Will Jackson Do?" *Commonweal* 115 (23 September 1988): 488.

95. Aristotle, *Politics,* 1274b32–1275b24; Robert Dahl, *Dilemmas of Pluralist Democracy* (New Haven: Yale University Press, 1982).

6

Thinking about Tomorrow Worriedly: The Election of 1992

And all the unsettled humours of the land ...
Have sold their fortunes at their native homes,
Bearing their birthrights proudly on their backs,
To make a hazard of new fortunes here.

— The Life and Death of King John (II, i)

Half a millennium ago, Columbus, unwitting, landed in a new world, and Americans in 1992 suspected that, like him, they had arrived at some unexpected place, full of unfamiliar shadows.* In the election, most Americans allowed themselves to be drawn by hope, but they went wistfully, driven by worries and without much confidence, convinced that they had more to fear than fear itself.

Change was in the air: for the first time in more than half a century, a presidential election was not framed by war, present or rumored; voters were restless; new concerns and constituencies made themselves felt; and the victorious Democrats pro-

---

* A century earlier, prophetically, Henry Adams saw the American people "wandering in a wilderness more sandy than ... Sinai," and in 1893, the Columbian Exposition seemingly "asked ... for the first time ... whether the American people knew where they were driving." Henry Adams, *The Education of Henry Adams,* ed. Ernest Samuels (Boston: Houghton Mifflin, 1974), 329, 343. But few Americans, back then, shared the vision.

claimed themselves a "new" party. Yet no election has so often or so pervasively been compared to the American past; Americans wanted assurance of comparability if not continuity, looking for old landmarks and fixed stars in the strange new world they confronted.

The election was likened to the contest in 1932 and to earlier third-party elections, especially the races in 1912, 1968, and 1980.* Observers drew parallels between Bush and other defeated incumbents—Taft, Carter, and most insistently, Herbert Hoover.[1] On the other side, analysts sought Clinton's prototype in Carter, in Kennedy, even in Franklin Roosevelt.[2] For obvious reasons, Clinton was not often compared to Truman, that tower of straight talk and private rectitude, but he did claim Truman's legacy. It was a heritage much in demand: Perot had designs on it and so, even more implausibly, did George Bush. Both comparisons were bizarre, and not only because Bush, a dutiful son of a Republican family, had voted for Dewey in 1948. Unlike Perot, Truman was a partisan and an insider, whose life was spent in the environs of politics and who never shook—or really sought to shake—his association with the Pendergast machine. And Truman, the come-from-behind campaigner Bush hoped to emulate, himself ran an almost completely partisan campaign, with few references to his opponent and no attacks on his character.[3] Lyndon Johnson, however, was not used as a model for the three candidates, although through Vietnam and racial politics he was a presence in the campaign; in 1992, Americans showed signs of making their peace with Johnson's lacerating failure and his equally troubling success.

In any event, a great many Americans, viewing the present, found themselves attracted to earlier times, especially to their

---

* Leslie Gelb, "1932 and 1992," *New York Times,* 7 February 1992, A29; R.W. Apple, Jr., "Close Three-Way Race Holds Opportunities for Clinton," *New York Times,* 23 June 1992, A18. Some voters compared their excitement with that of the first Roosevelt election, as they told Michael Winerip, "Fever Pitch: Democracy at Work," *New York Times,* 1 November 1992, E49.

moments of strength and exuberance. After the "numbness" of the presidential debates, Russell Baker wrote, "the mind finds itself shamefully yearning for a benighted time when vigor, sassiness, confidence, even arrogance, expressed itself in the national spirit."[4] In 1992, confidence did not point Americans to the future, it drew them to the past; and the election, a vote for change, was also a hope for renewal.

Economic Disorder and the American Civil Order

In one sense, the election is easily explained: Bush, R.W. Apple, Jr., noted, was "the economy's casualty."[5] The bad portents began to be apparent early on; by August 1991, Warren Brookes was arguing that the economy's woes might make Bush a "sitting duck" for the Democrats, and so it proved.[6] Democrats refused to be distracted and, in the end, achieved something close to their old fantasy, an election fought out simply on economic terms.*

The numbers were depressing. Unemployment was relatively high, job creation had virtually stopped, and the gross national product (GNP) was going nowhere.[7] Yet as Bush complained rather plaintively, the data were not *that* bad, especially when compared to other countries, and there were bright spots, such as low inflation and low interest rates.[8]

The greatest problem for the president lay behind the figures. Short-term calculations and immediate economic experiences, and even self-interest, narrowly defined, are less potent politically than judgments about the future and about the country as a whole.[9] In 1988, Bush had parroted Ronald Reagan's 1980 question, "Are you better off than you were four years

---

* For the hope, see Robert Kuttner, *The Life of the Party: Democratic Prospects in 1988 and Beyond* (New York: Viking, 1987); by contrast, cultural cleavages were dominant in 1988. Joel Lieske, "Cultural Issues and Images in the 1988 Presidential Campaign," *PS* 24 (1991): 180–87.

ago?" and the promise of improvement haunted him in 1992. But Reagan himself withstood worse economic conditions in the congressional elections of 1982, when the Republicans suffered relatively light losses because voters were convinced he had a star to steer by. In 1992, by contrast, the country felt no such assurance about times to come. Even during the Great Depression, Americans could take comfort in being the world's largest creditor, an industrial powerhouse with a favorable balance of trade and little public debt. All those consolations are now turned upside down, and the recession in 1992 differed from any since World War II "in the near certainty that it is not a prelude to any substantial recovery."[10]

Voters had been inclined to say that the country was on the "wrong track" even when Bush's ratings were high, and time only added to their pessimism.[11] Material well-being was only a part of the story: for many of the electorate in 1992, the economic issue was dignity for themselves and their country.

In the beginning of the Republic, Jefferson observed that virtually all free men could enjoy the degree of economic independence necessary to self-governing citizenship. He relied, in his familiar thesis, on the existence of abundant land, available to yeoman proprietors, but it was also important, he wrote later on, that even those who worked for wages could expect to find "comfortable subsistence" and the ability to provide for old age.[12] In the latter argument, the critical factor is not income, although Jefferson presumes a socially adequate wage; his case relies on the worker's confidence that he will be able to find work at "satisfactory" pay so that no worker feels unduly dependent on a particular employer. And through much of our history, with only a little distortion, Americans have been able to take that condition as the ordinary rule.

Contemporary Americans are less likely to enjoy that good fortune. Blue-collar labor, once a kind of aristocracy, has been watching its position deteriorate for years: the 1991 *Economic Report to the President* indicated that the average weekly wage of blue-collar workers had fallen 20 percent since 1972.[13]

Middle-class families generally have been able to keep incomes stable or rising, but only by relying on second wage earners, working longer hours, and borrowing, caught in the cycle of "work and spend."[14] More and more households, too, have found their health insurance threatened as employers seek to control costs.[15]

By a good many reckonings, the income of Americans in the middle sectors of society has been stagnant for a decade, and the U.S. Census Bureau recently noted a long-term decline in the percentage of Americans ranked in the middle class.[16] Inequality is growing, reaching "Great Gatsby levels," Paul Krugman says; even on the right, Charles Murray is troubled by the disparity between a considerable elite (10 to 20 percent) that can "bypass institutions it doesn't like" and the rest of the public, foreshadowing a society divided into the exempt and the trapped.[17]

During the Reagan years, this increase in inequality could be treated, in middle-class America, as only the other side of opportunity.* The recession of 1992, however, struck at the jobs of white-collar labor, its threat magnified by the fact that the middle class carries a burden of debt and expectations that makes its way of life exceptionally vulnerable.[18] Whole layers of management are disappearing, apparently for good, as companies strive to become "lean." Moreover, such jobs as are being created—blue and white collar—include a growing number of temporary positions, evidently less secure, with lower wages and benefits.†

Economic troubles, bad enough by themselves, were interwoven with concern for civil order and the decencies of private life. Despite devotion to "family values," the deterioration of

---

* As, to some extent, Mickey Kaus does in *The End of Equality* (New York: Basic Books, 1992).

† Hobart Rowen, "Misdiagnosing the Recession," *Washington Post National Weekly*, 27 January–12 February 1992), 5; Anne Swardson, "The Swelling Ranks of the Underemployed," *Washington Post National Weekly*, 17–23 February 1992, 20; Peter Passell, "Clinton's Luck ... Or Albatross?" *New York Times*, 13 August 1992, D2. It is a sign of

families escalated during the Reagan-Bush years: the number of single-parent households increased by almost 50 percent, and too many of those families are desperately poor, while even in economically better-off homes with two parents, the demands of work drain time and quality from family life.[19] At best, families are losing autonomy; the media begin to inculcate their "hidden curriculum" in infancy, before literacy and to some extent even before speech.* Visible in the media, if not in day-to-day life, divorce, feminism, and the demand for gay rights, to say nothing of new ethnic diversities, are undermining old certainties. Change and mobility continue to make us hesitant about commitments to persons and places, and in a more overtly sinister way, crime keeps citizens away from public spaces, barring doors when it does not prompt a retreat to some place of relative safety.[20] The affluent are inclined to seek private solutions and immunities, while the less fortunate have their own forms of privatization, most destructively in the autoanesthesia of drugs.[21] Too many Americans are alone, frightened, or uncivil, and all of us are at least a bit bewildered. Living in a state of anxious vulnerability, if not privation, multitudes of Americans in 1992 were disgusted with an administration that they saw as out of touch, indifferent, and ineffective.

Foreign policy, George Bush's strong suit, gave him little help. With some pride, the president argued that because of Republican successes, Americans could sleep without fear of nu-

---

the times that, by October 1991, more Americans, by a margin of over half a million, worked for government than in manufacturing. When Reagan took office, manufacturing led by 25 percent. Floyd Norris, "The Jobs Are in Government, Not Industry," *New York Times,* 6 September 1992, F1.

* Urie Bronfenbrenner, "Contexts of Child Rearing," *American Psychologist* 34 (1979): 844–50; 74 percent of Americans, in one finding, consider that parents should have the greatest impact on their children's values, but a substantial plurality think that the media exert that influence. American Enterprise Public Opinion and Demographic Report, in *Public Perspective* 3 (September/October 1992): 86.

clear war, but that claim moved few voters.* The collapse of Soviet communism softened the glue that had held the conservative coalition together, and for most Americans, foreign threats
seemed distant, hypothetical, or unpersuasive.[22] In August, Bush
tried a little showy "toughness" with Iraq, but no other "October surprise" materialized, apart from the self-wounding search
through the Clintons' passport files. Possibly the administration
realized that, as Leslie Gelb observed, presidents "have so often
abused the national interest for their own political ends" that
Americans have come to take partisan purposes for granted.[23]
Disillusionment hovered even around Bush's triumph in the Gulf
war, which appeared more and more suspect and inconclusive, a
mood typified by the bumper stickers that read *Saddam Has a
Job. Do You?*[24]

In fact, foreign policy added to the American sense of economic and civic vulnerability. American borders are now perme-
ated by foreign products, capital, and labor.[25] Foreign governments, too, play increasingly evident roles in American politics,
as Ross Perot, with some exaggeration, so often observed. In
1988, Kevin Phillips claims, the Bank of Japan helped Bush so
much "it should have registered as a Republican political action
committee," and this year, the Miyazawa government, similarly
inclined, ordered Japanese companies to ship fewer cars to the
United States than they were allowed under Japan's self-imposed
quota.† Americans became accustomed to hearing that their
economy is no longer "world class," and already wounded by
slighting comments from Japanese leaders, they were not reas-

---

* Bush used the image of untroubled sleep so often that reporters
began referrint to the theme as "bedtime in America," parodying Reagan's "morning in America" slogan.

† Kevin Phillips, "The Old Boys' Club of the West Is Getting Left
in the Dust," *Washington Post National Weekly,* 13–19 July 1992, 23;
Hobart Rowen, "A Little Help from His Friends," *Washington Post National Weekly,* 20–26 April 1992, 5; Benjamin Ginsberg and Martin
Shefter describe "alliances with foreign governments" as one of the new
modes of politics, in *Politics by Other Means: The Declining Importance
of Elections in America* (New York: Basic Books, 1990), 11.

sured by Bush's feckless assertiveness in Tokyo, which came across as "bashing on bended knee."[26]

Clinton, an internationalist and, in these days, a moderate hawk, demonstrated a respectable aptitude for foreign policy, and many observers ended by sharing Gelb's verdict that Bush, an able leader in dealing with the "old security and power issues," was not up to the economic concerns that now occupy center stage in international politics.[27]

The Skeptical Search for an Active Government

The clearest message of 1992 was the majority's demand for active government, engaged to relieve America's discontents and reclaim the future. Even in 1988, opinion had tended to side with the candidate who, on any given issue, supported the use of public power.[28] This time, the tide was unmistakable: 62 percent voted for the differing, but undeniably activist persuasions of Clinton and Perot.

It was a hard year for laissez-faire. Rhetorically, the high point of the Democratic campaign was Mario Cuomo's attack on Bush for relying on "the invisible hand of some cyclical economic god" to save the ship of state, and less elegantly, the Democratic campaign featured denunciations of "trickle-down economics." * Even conservatives, of course, now accept a considerable degree of economic intervention: Ronald Reagan promised a "safety net," the Reagan and Bush administrations committed billions to protect depositors in failing banks and savings and loans, and the administration took it for granted that the Federal Reserve should manage interest rates to promote growth.† In 1992, the current of activism ran even

---

    * That the phrase hurt is indicated by Bush's effort to counter it by referring to "trickle-down" government.

    † Similarly, while Michael Novak rejects "socialist" versions of health insurance, he argued for a national plan based on tax credits. "Dead but Fair," *Forbes,* 16 March 1992, 112–13.

stronger. Among economists, there was something of a generational shift, reminiscent of the advent of Keynes, with practice brought to the critique of economic theory.* Clinton found no shortage of economists willing to agree, for example, that government is needed to promote saving and investment, especially since Reagan's reliance on the classical "equivalence theorem" —that government spending will lead to private saving—had proved misplaced.† By itself, moreover, investment may not be enough: counter to much conventional wisdom, there is good evidence that American productivity is not low. The problem may be that relative efficiency is being purchased at the price of employment, and so that government is needed to link investment, productivity, and work.[29]

Americans were only a little less likely to look to government to shore up the social and moral foundations of society or to build new ones. Most were inclined to think that government should support the family in some way or other.‡ Conservative noise about family should not obscure the fact that liberals, though they differ in their definitions of the family and the policies they recommend, are eager to extend help.[30] The willingness to involve government in civil life extends beyond the family: the communitarian movement has attracted support from a

---

* Steven Pearlstein, "First, Let's Kill All the Economists," *Washington Post National Weekly*, 30 November–5 December 1992, 31, cites Paul Krugman, "for people in their fifties, the cutting edge of economics was to show how markets were perfect. For people in their thirties, the cutting edge ... is now showing how markets are imperfect." See also Leonard Silk, "Is Liberalism Back in the Saddle?" *New York Times*, 17 April 1992, D2.

† Frank Levy and Richard Michel, *The Economic Future of American Families* (Washington, D.C.: Urban Institute, 1991); on the failure of the equivalence theorem, see Leonard Silk, "The Crucial Issue Politicians Ignore," *New York Times*, 24 April 1992, D2.

‡ According to the American Enterprise Public Opinion and Demographic Report, 68 percent said candidates should talk about family values; 53 percent said government should concern itself. *Public Perspective* 3 (September/October 1992): 85.

broad spectrum of intellectuals, while in practice, 1992 saw several states attempt to link welfare rights with obligations.* Even the vogue of environmental protection, limits to growth, and historic preservation, while often tied to fairly narrow self-interest, also reflects an effort to enlist policy on the side of community.[31]

This is part of an old story, for conservatism's concern for "values," often bigoted and bumbling, touches a truth. Government by itself cannot make us good, but it can encourage decency by reducing its costs and by raising the price of indecent behavior.[32] In America, that role of government has been vital: our customs and culture are not immemorial, but the result of a more or less conscious design, a people engaged in making itself.† American culture has been a perennially political issue, so it is no surprise that the contemporary "culture war" finds its way into democratic politics.[33] In fact, we ought to hope that the conflict can be expressed in, and confined to, democratic forms.

Unfortunately, our confidence on the point cannot be very great. Although Americans turned to government in 1992, they distrusted it and were apt to despise politics; a year earlier, Peter Hart and Douglas Bailey found that although voters "desperately want to believe in government," they were deeply disillusioned, so there was a "dangerously broad gulf between the governors and the governed."[34]

All our public pillars were more or less damaged.[35] Congress, which never stood too well with the public, was injured

---

* Peter Steinfels, "A Political Movement Blends Its Ideas from Left and Right," *New York Times,* 24 May 1991, E6; "in providing for the poor," *Commonweal* editorialized, "we must make reasonable demands on them—for work, schooling and, yes, sexual responsibility," 24 February 1992, 5. See also Christopher Jencks, *Rethinking Social Policy: Race, Poverty, and the Underclass* (Cambridge, Mass.: Harvard University Press, 1992).

† G.K. Chesterton noted that "what is unique is not America, but what is called Americanisation." *What I Saw in America* (New York: Dodd-Mead, 1922), 14.

by legislative delay, the "scandal" at the House bank, and most of all, by the hearings on Justice Clarence Thomas's confirmation. Watching Thomas and Anita Hill before the Judiciary Committee, voters divided on the basis of gender and class, but virtually all felt contempt for politicians, and David Rohde saw the hearings as one event in the long-term "undermining of respect for institutions."[36]

Historically, the presidency has been less exposed to scorn than Congress, but a long series of abuses—Watergate, Iran-*contra,* and what the media began to call "Iraqgate"—has worked its hurt. Carter's perceived failure left its weight of doubt, as did Reagan's increasingly evident ineptitude, and George Bush never had Reagan's teflon charm.[37]

The decline of political parties, of course, has long been apparent, and this year the low level of partisan allegiance was reflected in the oscillation of the polls.[38] Voters, seeing money as dominant in elections and increasingly convinced that corruption is the political rule, feel a lack of voice and representation; in a 1990 *Times-Mirror* poll, 57 percent of respondents agreed that "people like me don't have any say about what government does."[39] This mood of disaffiliation and deauthorization in turn encourages citizens to look outside the institutions or to the negations of protest politics, a disposition especially clear among those attracted to Ross Perot—a candidate by "immaculate conception," Garry Wills said, untainted by politics.[40] Perot voters, Richard Morin and E.J. Dionne, Jr., found, had no good words for political parties, and while a large number expressed a desire for a third party, they did so not because of any positive convictions or any confidence in democratic politics, but simply because they were applying a free-market model *to* politics, relying on the logic of competition.[41]

It was to be expected, then, that along with some hope, the electorate harbored an abiding doubt that government can succeed.[42] And although it has been almost twenty-five years since an active president dealt with a legislature of the same party—in many ways, Carter was suspect on both counts—the voters' lack of confidence is not simply instrumental. It reflects an accentuated mistrust of government's moral title and the suspicion that politicians have no goal except self-perpetuation.[43] Divided government, after all, has been the creation of distrust, the mirror of deauthorization.* It also set in motion its own vicious cycle: the voters' disaffiliation has made leaders shy away from any policies with immediate costs, resulting in a "no pain" politics, full of posturings, such as the Balanced Budget Amendment, frustrating for leaders and citizens alike.[44] Political leaders have become more contemptuous of the electorate, not always so secretly, while the voters—on a generous reading—were left with a "grumpy cynicism."[45]

The prevailing discontents made it all the more striking that voter turnout in 1992 reversed the long decline in participation.[46] That the race was apparently closing undoubtedly helped, as did the fact that so many voters felt themselves immediately threatened by the recession. These factors, more or less specific to 1992, suggest that voters may easily lapse into their old indifference; over the long haul, individuals calculating self-interested utilities will find only inadequate reasons for going to the polls. Consistent participation presumes a fuller involvement in community life.† The signal in 1992 was faint, but Americans did hint that they are willing to be drawn back into the political system by any relatively entertaining show.[47]

---

* I am not persuaded by the notion that divided government is "accidental." See James Sundquist, "Needed: A Political Theory for the New Era of Coalition Government in the U.S.," *Political Science Quarterly* 103 (1988): 633–34. The more purposive model implied by Morris Fiorina in *Divided Government* (New York: Macmillan, 1992), 128–29, is more compelling, especially since divided government need not result in "gridlock" and did not do so under Nixon. See also David Mayhew, *Divided We Govern* (New Haven: Yale University Press, 1991).

† Gerald Pomper and Loretta Sernekos, "Bake Sales and Voting," *Society*, July/August 1991, 10–16. Tocqueville argued that Americans were driven into politics by necessity but held there by the habits and pleasures of community life. See *Democracy in America* (New York: Schocken, 1961), 2:127.

Public Life and Private Politics

Clinton's great challenge, and the Republic's, lies in the need to strengthen the dignity of citizenship and the quality of democratic consent. Knowing this, Clinton plans something approximating a permanent campaign, but the media, a part of his intended solution, are an even bigger part of the political problem.

Earlier in our history, Alexis de Tocqueville had no doubt that the press was an essentially representative institution, deriving much of its authority from the power of communities to hold it accountable. Like the media we know, the press of Tocqueville's day was inclined to slight principles in favor of personalities and to pursue public figures into their private lives. Tocqueville saw a press, however, that was local and intimate with its readers, enjoying less power than a mass press, but more authority, so that it was less likely to "give way to the current of the multitude."[48] Bound up with its communities, Tocqueville thought, the press was better able to instruct them and might even suggest from time to time that private and local interests should yield to the public good.[49] The "old news," Bill Moyers writes in the same spirit, "drew people to the public square" and helped teach the "vital habits of democracy."[50]

In contemporary America, in contrast, the dominant forms of the press are media by which information is communicated *to* us, but without any serious element of reciprocity or accountability.[51] We depend on the media and recognize their power, but our dependence is a mark of voicelessness and indignity.[52]

Recognizing our resentment and their lack of authority, the media are desperately anxious to please us, as Tocqueville would have expected, especially since few things are easier than changing channels. But in the first place, that disposition makes the media contemptible and incapable of self-regulation without limiting their power. In 1992, for example, the media's early resolution to forego sensational inquiries into the private lives of candidates crumbled under the impact of the supermarket tabloids, and the whole of the press was soon engaged in what one

British paper called "sexual McCarthyism."[53] Similarly, concerned with criticism of the ever-shortening "sound bite"—
down to 7.3 seconds, by one calculation, in 1988—CBS decided
that all sound bites would, henceforth, be 30 seconds or more.
But news editors, reaching the conclusion that such "bites" were
unavailable or "unwieldy," eliminated them almost altogether,
showing reporters more and candidates less.[54] And second, even
the determination of *how* to please us is made by the media, on
the basis of criteria and evidence they choose. This unauthorized
decision making fuels the fear of some secret political design. In
1992, conservatives were particularly apt to detect a hostile con-
spiracy, or at least a tilt to the left, but plenty of liberals heard a
tune called by Republican elites.* In fact, the media are probably shaped less by political intent than by "mass circulation
images, themselves squeezed by commercial pressures," a principle just as troubling.[55]

The opinions that guide the media are not genuinely public,
though they come from the people. The media reach us in private settings and address largely private concerns and feelings,
relying on images more than words.† Where radio, as Russell
Baker remembers, "intoxicated us with voices," the contemporary media discount speech, continuing the grand modern impulse, initiated by Machiavelli, to exalt the visible and nonver-
bal, the deed as opposed to the word.[56] To the extent that they

---

* Harvey Mansfield refers to a "tendency toward the left." See
America's Constitutional Soul (Baltimore: Johns Hopkins University Press,
1991), 167. By contrast, Deborah Tannen refers to the news media as manipulated by "mostly Republican" admakers in a review of Kathleen Hall
Jamieson, *Dirty Politics* (New York: Oxford University Press, 1992).
"Lies, Damned Lies and Political Ads," *Washington Post National Weekly,*
21–27 September 1992, 35.

† Mansfield, *America's Constitutional Soul,* 166–68. In an admittedly extreme example in 1990, Madonna, wrapped in an American flag,
urged young Americans to vote on the principle that "freedom of speech is
as good as sex," thus identifying public words with private passions and
justifying the former in terms of the latter. *New York Times,* 20 October
1990, 7.

are treated by the media at all, political speech and deliberation are presented as a kind of theater of deception, in which content matters only as clue to covert forces and schemes. In response to the president's State of the Union message, John Tierney noted that "the chief question raised by analysts on television was not whether his proposals made any sense, but how the Democrats would respond to his staff's strategy."[57]

This year, American resentment of the media turned so explosive that suddenly the campaign was dominated by "new" news—"weird media," Bush said—the talk shows and tabloids, Don Imus and Arsenio Hall, Larry King and the "infomercial."[58] Ross Perot was the first to see the advantages of the new vehicles; Clinton, damaged by the more orthodox media, soon followed. The new media have undeniable benefits: they are apt to be free, and they allow candidates to develop positions in depth, or at length, at any rate. Clinton turned to them in some relief. After a frustrating, much-trivialized primary in New York, Clinton sought to use his victory speech to direct public attention to the substance of his campaign, but after four minutes, all the networks except for CNN and C-Span stopped their coverage, and CNN dropped out after nine minutes. Network news reduced the speech to sound bites, and the next morning, on the "Today Show," Clinton's remarks had been shrunk to "I love Wisconsin, Minnesota and Kansas, and I really love New York."[59] The talk shows, by contrast, allowed Clinton to display his virtuosity and command of the issues.[60] The new media, moreover, worked to diminish the advantage the party in power draws from its ability to dominate television news, and Republicans can be expected to cultivate them in force in 1996.[61]

For viewers, what mattered in the "new news" was face-to-face interaction with hosts and with audiences, or hearing candidates field called-in questions, an approximation, even if weak, of town-meeting democracy. But the "community," produced for the media, is only another image that can be managed. It comes into being around and because of leaders—the hosts or their guests—so that the talk shows only emphasize, as

Ellen Hume put it, "that the media are our new political bosses —the direct filter that parties used to be."[62] The media audience cannot hold its studio "representatives" accountable, nor can the individuals who make up the "community" of questioners speak to one another without the assistance of the media themselves. The "electronic town hall," Gerald Marzorati wrote, is what passes for civic community when people live among strangers and the "friendliest colleagues are the computer, database and fax."[63] The new media, in sum, did not renew American citizenship, although they may have made citizenship seem interesting; as David Broder noted early on, they offered only the "catharsis" of "highly contrived dramas."[64]

Nothing in 1992 changed the fact that masses of Americans, inundated with information, know they lack the means of separating the false from the true.* As Michael Rogin argues, all too many citizens find themselves facing a baffling, overwhelming, and often arcane government in the "paranoid position" of "disordering powerlessness" and are tempted to equally paranoid analysis.[65] They are nudged further in that direction by the media's blurring of the line between politics and fiction, exemplified by the rise of the docudrama and movies like Oliver Stone's *JFK*.† This aspect of the media weakens the check of reality and encourages "splitting," the psychological process by which heroes or times past are idealized—as with John Kennedy

---

* And politically, the truth matters. Intellectual champions of the view that reality is "constructed" and "plural" did not apply their teaching to the verdict constructed by the jury that tried the officers who arrested and beat Rodney King. "Postmodernists," Todd Gitlin writes, "enjoy skating on the surface, but they, we, are still probing for bedrock truth." Gitlin, "On Being Sound-Bitten," 17. On the King verdict, see Jeffrey Frank, "When Truth Becomes Image, History Becomes Myth," *Washington Post National Weekly*, 11–17 May 1992, 24.

† Caryl Rivers, "It's Tough to Tell a Hawk from a Lonesome Dove," *New York Times*, 10 February 1991, H29ff. We need to remember the spectacle of the vice-president of the United States in national dialogue with fictional TV characters. See Russell Baker, "To Cloud Men's Minds," *New York Times*, 23 May 1992, Y15.

or the "inheritance" denied to young Americans—while their negative qualities are disowned and identified with demonized and conspiratorial enemies.[66]

There were plenty of examples in 1992. Ross Perot, pushing aside evidence of his own use of investigators and personal threats, as well as his dealings with foreign governments, talked a good deal about the plots of Republican dirty tricksters and foreign agents in major-party campaigns.[67] Most pervasively, however, homosexuals—as Rogin pointed out—were identified with erotic and social disorder; this was true of the leftist fantasy of Oliver Stone, of the falangist rhetoric of Patrick Buchanan on the right, and of Perot's fear that appointing a gay cabinet member would cause "controversy" or that his daughter might be portrayed as a lesbian.

There was no shortage of Americans who, sharing such persuasions, were eager for a leader able to cut through the thicket of democratic politics. And others, less troubled, shared the same impatience.

The candidacy of Ross Perot epitomized many of the themes of 1992, but it would have been impossible without the media. On their battlefield, Perot proved a master strategist. He opened and promoted his candidacy through talk shows, trailing a stream of one-liners; he demonstrated the viability of the "infomercial"; and week by week, he spent more money purchasing time for his interrupted campaign than any previous candidate.[68] Perot showed that with grand salesmanship and enough money it is possible to become a major force without passing through the primaries or the parties, and dodging the press where he could not dominate it, he avoided almost all the scrutiny that goes with a traditional campaign.[69]

Of course, even Perot could not entirely sidestep the old modes, and Perot the candidate repeatedly undermined Perot the strategist, revealing too much of his testy, autocratic, and paranoid streak.[70] Yet at the beginning of the campaign, Perot was able to present himself as a candidate of force who could solve all problems magically, virtually without cost—"without breaking a sweat," as he liked to say—and otherwise, as a tabula rasa on which voters could write their own scripts and fantasies.[71]

Recognition that ending the deficit would call for taxes and for sacrifice of a high order helped persuade Perot to quit the race.[72] When he returned, he retained the image of "can do" forcefulness, now combined with a "message" that—vague in so many details—was presented as complete and tied to Perot's persona.[73]

The common thread of Perot's two campaigns was his demand for quick solutions and his unwillingness to do the prolonged work of persuasion and compromise within institutions. Hostility to institutions, in fact, was a major part of his appeal. In May, the great majority of Bush and Clinton supporters, while critical of Congress generally, approved the job being done by their own House members, but 55 percent of those supporting Perot disapproved.[74] That unhappiness fit neatly with Perot's discounting of representative government and his disdain for conflicts of interest and party, the messy charms of democratic politics.[75] The instinct of the entrepreneur, Michael Schrage observed, is the desire to create new forms, and hence to reject established institutions; Perot had the special attraction of an "outsider" who was knowledgeable about the system, one who did not offer to dismantle government but promised to make it stronger and more effective.[76] In addition, the nationalism of his antiforeign themes amounted to a pledge to restore the American imperium as a part of America's inheritance.

Repeatedly, Perot's campaign was linked to the "tradition of prairie populism," but the stark differences between his movement and the old Populism illustrate the difficulties of contemporary democratic life.[77] The Populists of 1892 grew out of and were composed of a dense forest of membership groups and face-to-face communities, so the People's Party was a federation of localities and associations, held close to the grass roots.* The

---

*   Lawrence Goodwyn, *Democratic Promise* (New York: Oxford University Press, 1976); the St. Louis Conference, early in 1892, seated delegates of twenty-two separate organizations. John Hicks, *The Populist Revolt* (Minneapolis: University of Minnesota Press, 1931), 225.

party abounded in policies, many spelled out in detailed plans: The Sub-Treasury system; free silver; the graduated income tax; the government ownership of railroads, telegraph, and tele phone were only the most prominent.*

But the Populists of 1892 had trouble finding a candidate. Their best bet, Polk of North Carolina, died before the convention, and Judge Walter Gresham turned them down. In the end, they nominated a veteran but rather uninspiring radical, General James B. Weaver, more or less because "there was little else left to do."[78]

By contrast, Perot's movement was constructed from the top down, its organization at least inspired and certainly sustained by Perot's money. It offered few policies; only the deficit-reduction program, the centerpiece of the second campaign, had much solidity. Above all, Perot's movement was centered on and defined by its candidate. Even Perot's version of the "electronic town hall," George Will pointed out, involved citizens giving information to the leader, not discussing or making decisions among themselves—an image, Will thought, shaped by the mystique of leadership with which Woodrow Wilson had invested the presidency.†

"I'm doing this for the American people," Perot often declared, "because they can't do it for themselves." Just so. Whatever the legacy of Perot's candidacy, it pointed to our distance from Populism's promise and to the endangered status of democratic citizenship.

---

* Matthew Josephson, a bit disdainful of the Populists as a party of "peasant proprietors," noted that "principles and platform" were central to them. *The Politicos* (New York: Harcourt, Brace, 1938), 502–3.

† George Will, "Ross Perot: America's Rohrschach Test," *Washington Post National Weekly*, 8–14 June 1992, 29. Perot's third-party candidacy thus violated Lowi's crucial "proviso" that such a party be built "from bottom up." Lowi, "The Party Crasher," *New York Times Magazine*, 23 August 1992, 33.

The State of the Political Parties

Perot's candidacy, of course, also testified to discontent with the nominating process. In droves, voters rejected the primary system, grumbling about the choices offered and staying away from the polls. Many, a plurality at one point, found themselves supporting Perot despite the fact that he had avoided primaries altogether. The system, Russell Baker wrote, "is dead, dead, dead and ought to be buried before it kills the two major parties." *

Baker's obituary was premature. The primary system was wounded, but it will survive, especially because the Democrats won the election. Bush's nomination made many voters unhappy, but they saw that it was more or less inevitable; Clinton's candidacy was the source of more murmuring, and his success will quiet many critics.

Yet Clinton did emerge from the primary season as a flawed candidate, so damaged by doubts about his character that crowds of Democrats would have preferred someone else, just as they would have done when campaigning began.† The primary system, however, forced candidates to choose early, when Bush looked like a sure winner. The leading Democrats opted to wait for more likely times, leaving the field to long-shot players. Mario Cuomo might have entered relatively late in the game, but he took himself out, and the Democrats were left with the candidates in the field. The primary system has enough residual democratic legitimacy to prevent the party conventions from setting aside the verdict of its long string of elections.‡

---

* Russell Baker, "Stressed All Over," *New York Times,* 6 June 1992, A23; R.W. Apple, Jr., "The Voters' Message," *New York Times,* 8 April 1992. Even Edward Kearny and Robert Heineman, who predicted a centrist third party, overestimated the attachment of voters to the primaries. "Scenario for a Centrist Revolt: Third Party Prospects in a Time of Ideological Polarization," *Presidential Studies Quarterly* 22 (1992): 114.

† It sometimes seemed that Democrats would be better off with a generic "Brand X" candidate. Robin Toner, "Bad News for Bush as Poll Shows National Gloom," *New York Times,* 28 January 1992, A1ff.

‡ Cuomo certainly received plenty of advice akin to Leslie Gelb's counsel to wait for 1996, using the time to cope with his "inner demons."

The primaries gave the Democrats two consolations in 1992. In the first place, President Bush was also scarred by Pat Buchanan's challenge. Moved to confess that he had made a "mistake" in agreeing to higher taxes, Bush added evident weakness to the sin of broken promises. And the president and his advisers responded curiously to the returns. In New Hampshire and after, Buchanan's supporters were mostly independents intent on "sending a message," voters who crossed the ideological spectrum. Bush, however, seemed to hear only the clamor on the right, setting a pattern for the campaign.[79]

Second, although the primaries ended with Perot ascendant and the Democrats near desperation, Clinton proved a supremely resilient candidate who played his hand well. Happy with the result, Democrats need to remember that Clinton's nomination was itself a chancy business, since it turned on Jesse Jackson's decision to stay out of the race and on the fact that Governor Douglas Wilder did not prove to be a viable candidate. Everywhere, Clinton had a decisive advantage among black voters, and that edge was critical to his victories. Had he lost those votes to Jackson or another African American candidate, he might have done no better on Super Tuesday than Senator Al Gore did in 1988, when Jackson won some southern primaries and Michael Dukakis squeaked by in Texas and Florida.[80] In this sense, Jackson, absent, was still a master spirit. His decision to forego the primaries allowed Clinton to build a class coalition across racial lines, the foundation for his success in November.

The Democrats have always been the more fractious party, a coalition of localities, ethnicities, and interests full of inner conflict and including ancient enemies united only by a sense of exclusion and opposition to the status quo. The GOP ordinarily

---

"To Cuomo or Not to Cuomo," *New York Times,* 27 November 1991, A21. Since the Democratic nomination is not likely to be doubtful in 1996, it might be a noncontroversial time to institutionalize Terry Sanford's proposal for a preprimary convention of superdelegates to screen candidates. See Walter Mondale's fine critique of primaries, "Primaries Are No Test of Character," *New York Times,* 26 February 1992, A23.

has more positive bonds, with the defense of the established order—especially the private economy—as the party's bottom
line.*

Social Issues: The Democrats and Race

For contemporary Democrats, race has been the bittersweet
apple of discord. This is not an entirely new story, since Democrats began to lose support in the South in the 1940s; but since
1964, Democratic championship of blacks and other minorities
has led to defections that have been nationwide, chronic, and
ordinarily decisive in presidential elections. Liberal Democrats
did not acknowledge quickly enough that middle- and working-
class whites were bearing a disproportionate part of the social
and economic burden of the quest for equality, and their failure
to redistribute those costs made it seem, to many traditional
Democrats, that the party had deserted them in favor of minorities on one hand and liberal elites on the other.[81] And Republicans have been forward and effective in cultivating that view.

In 1992, however, race was a dog that did not bark, noteworthy for its relative absence as an issue in the campaign. In
the second presidential debate, Carole Simpson had to prod her
audience to ask about the politics of race, and even her insistence brought only a vapid inquiry about how soon minorities
or women might be elected president or vice-president. The si-
lence was more evident because the occasions of racial conflict
were so thunderous: the rioting in Los Angeles that followed the
verdict in the trial of the police officers who had arrested and
beaten Rodney King, only an extreme case of urban ethnic conflict, forced more insulated Americans to look, briefly, at the
ravaged ground and human desperation of the inner city. The
sight was so dreadful that most Americans were happy to turn

---

* With both parties, this is an old tradition. See Herbert Croly,
"Democratic Factions and Insurgent Republicans," *North American Review* 191 (May 1910): 626–35.

to something else, while for Americans of all races, economic conditions helped to discount other concerns.[82]

More specifically political factors were also at work. Ron Brown's visibility as national chairman symbolized the fact, recognized by an increasing number of African Americans, that blacks are no longer outsiders pressuring Democrats, but the new regulars, the heart of the party.[83] That perception strengthened the impulse, at least among leaders and activists, to find common ground, and with it, a willingness to speak the language of class rather than race.[84] Some of the most compelling African American voices showed themselves uneasy with the old shibboleths.[85] For Democrats of all races, moreover, the Los Angeles riots emphasized the need to win, making ideology less compelling than the need to end the decade of neglect, to do something to ease the agony of the inner city and the sense of superfluity that is the most terrible affliction of the underclass. It was part of the temper of 1992 that a surprisingly wide spectrum of African American leaders supported the principle that, just as all citizens have contributions to make, public assistance is rightly tied to responsibilities.* Clinton, William Julius Wilson wrote, spoke to "those who have grown weary of destructive racial rhetoric," and this year, that disposition counted.[86]

It allowed Clinton to distance himself from Sister Souljah and from Jesse Jackson, a decisive gesture to "Reagan Democrats," without any significant loss of support from African Americans.† Although not enough blacks went to the polls,

---

* Lena Williams, "Growing Black Debate on Racism: When Is It Real, When an Excuse," *New York Times*, 5 April 1992, 1ff. "To join the public household of this great nation," Orlando Patterson wrote after the election, "is to share responsibility for its fortunes and for one's failings." "Our History vs. Clinton's Covenant," *New York Times*, 13 November 1992, A29.

† It helped, of course, that Bush's record on the politics of race showed a combination of indifference and backsliding, while Perot was clearly impossible after his early gaffes. Ruth Marcus, "The Shifting Sands of George Bush's Civil Rights Positions," *Washington Post National Weekly*, 24–30 August 1992, 8–9.

Clinton gathered the percentage of support among African Americans that Democrats have come to expect, in part because, whatever his other maneuvers, he addressed and appealed to their dignity as citizens.[87] Intermittently, in Clinton's rhetoric, there were intimations of a Republic of equals.

Social Issues: The Republicans and Religion

Where the Democrats achieved a reasonable degree of unity, the Republicans called attention to their most troublesome divisions. The Reagan years made the GOP more discordant; its new accessions of strength, especially among social conservatives and the religious right, are also occasions for quarrel. The old rift between Main Street and Wall Street was, in large measure, a difference of interest; the new dissensions are matters of faith and culture.*

This year's Republican convention, the party's opening to the nation at large, was more or less given over to the cultural right. Its stridency, mirrored in the early part of the Bush campaign, presented Republicans in a role that, since 1964, had been claimed most often by Democrats, a party captured by ideologues and zealots.[88] The prominence of the right helped fracture the Republican coalition: In 1988, 90 percent of Republican voters supported Bush, but in 1992, his share fell to 73 percent, most of the defectors going to Perot.[89]

Still, while the Republicans ran a maladroit campaign, marked by arrogance and misjudgment, their strategists had reason to think that a turn to the right and an emphasis on "family values" was their best alternative.[90] Bush, always a poor candidate, was saddled with the stumbling economy, and it made matters worse that, by pledging to make voters "better off," he

---

* William Schneider, "The Political Legacy of the Reagan Years," in *The Reagan Legacy,* edited by Sidney Blumenthal and Thomas Byrne Edsall (New York: Pantheon, 1988), 12. At that, Republican divisions are probably less severe than those among Democrats. Corwin Smidt and James Penning, "A Party Divided?" *Polity* 23 (1990): 138.

had invited them to desert him in hard times.[91] Unlike Reagan, Bush has no gift for political poetry. He is guided by certain working rules good manners, confidence in the market economy, and devotion to the national interest—but, notoriously, he regards the "vision thing" as a word-spinning disturbance to the logic of practice, propriety, and power.[92] In 1988, Dukakis's emphasis on "competence" allowed Bush to present himself as the candidate of principles, but that opportunity was not offered in 1992, and in fact, Bush frequently seemed to be a weather vane, pointing in whatever direction he was blown by opinion or perceived political advantage.[93]

Needing an appeal that would be proof against economic distress, at a time when foreign policy no longer galvanized voters, Bush and his advisers fell back on the social issues. Bush's dependence on the right was greater, and the risks of that dependence smaller, in a three-way race, since Perot had already shaken Republican loyalties.[94] Despite all of Bush's liabilities, it was the right that kept him in the race: In 1992, the core support of the Republicans came from social conservatives, and the party will need their loyalty in the years to come.[95]

To assemble a winning coalition, the Republicans will need to moderate their stance on social issues, but doing so will call for art and delicacy. Social conservatives cannot be taken for granted: evangelical Protestants—and even more, socially conservative Catholics—can lean to the left on economic questions, and many might change sides if they feel abandoned, especially since Clinton keeps an open door.[96] Even in 1992, while white, born-again Christians heavily supported Bush, Clinton did better than Dukakis, winning about one vote in four, where Dukakis received only one in five.[97]

Paradoxically, the need for moderation points the Republicans right and not left. Bush had to curry favor with the right, stepping up his rhetoric where Reagan could be temperate because, unlike Reagan, the right did not see Bush as one of its own.[98] After all, in 1984, Bush had confessed his discomfort with the "elevation of the religion thing," and in practice, his support for the right-wing agenda had been modest at best.* Feeling its oats in 1992, the right made Bush pay the price. If Republicans want to lower that cost in 1996, they will need a candidate who is pragmatic but is perceived by the right as one of its champions, and that may be a tall order to fill.

On the other side, Democrats have reason to pause amid their ecstasies. Clinton's skillful race still fell far short of a national majority, and his victory can be explained by third-candidate defections more than any increase in Democratic strength.

Republican hopes of realignment were blunted. A higher percentage of college students began calling themselves liberal, and there was much comment about Clinton's appeal to the young.[99] But in the end, about the same percentage of younger voters went for Clinton as had gone Democratic four years earlier, while among younger married voters with children, Clinton did very badly indeed.[100] On the other hand, he apparently won an overwhelming majority among homosexuals.[101] Still, comparing Democratic support in 1988 and 1992, change was the exception and continuity the rule.

The Emerging American Politics

Clinton's victory, however, hinted at broader possibilities for redefining the Democratic coalition. On election night, Al Gore asserted that the election demonstrated the "end of sectionalism," and in a sense, it did confirm sectionalism's long decline.[102] But Clinton's southernness still made him seem alien to many northern audiences, and even Gore's argument pointed to the special sectional character of the Democratic ticket.[103] As the nomination of two border staters, it was not unprecedented; rather, it turned away from Dukakis's effort to re-create the Boston-Austin axis to that earlier success, the Truman-Barkley

---

* Alan Geyer identifies Bush with "political docetism," a creed of vague, disembodied values. See *Christianity and Crisis,* 21 September 1992, 291; David Broder, "Value Added Politics," *Washington Post National Weekly,* 1–7 June 1992, 4.

ticket of 1948. But unlike those predecessors, Clinton and Gore came from states that were members of the Confederacy: the 1992 nominations were a strong symbolic gesture to the South, part of a successful effort to dent that now-Republican bastion.*

The geography of the election was suggestive in another way. Sweeping the Northeast and the West Coast, Clinton and Gore also were almost universally successful in the broad, middle American region that Meredith Nicholson once called the "Valley of Democracy."[104] Except for Mississippi, Clinton carried every state bordering on the Mississippi River and every state on the Ohio except Indiana, equaling Lyndon Johnson (who took Indiana but lost Louisiana).† Only on the upper Missouri did Clinton's pluralities disappear.

Our stereotypes associate the two areas with the Democratic Party's fundamental agon. We think of the coasts—somewhat unjustly, of course—as the homeland of liberals and neoliberals, a diverse grouping uniting partisans of high-tech industry and the cultural elite, mostly internationalists disposed toward free trade, almost all secular and inclined to relativism, people who defend policies in the idiom of rights.[105] Middle America, by contrast, symbolizes those in the middle sectors who "do the work, raise the kids, and pay the bills," the people to whom Clinton offered himself as champion and who probably gave him his margin of victory. For all their variety, these middle Americans are often tied to place and apt to be religious, not often moralists (at least, not those who voted for Clinton), but concerned with decency and justice—with families and safe communities and fair taxes—at least as much as they care about rights. And less confident about international politics, they include many unashamed patriots who sympathize with protection.[106]

---

* Bush helped by calling Arkansas "the lowest of the low" in the third debate, which to sensitive ears, sounded like regional and class contempt. *New York Times,* 1 November 1992, A1.

† Even in Mississippi, Clinton carried all the counties that touch the river except Warren and De Soto, if county-by-county maps are accurate.

The "character issue" chafed the line of friction between the two persuasions. The most bothersome side of Clinton's account of his doings during the Vietnam era was not that he tried to avoid military service—as the warm reception to his American Legion speech showed, that could have been dealt with rather easily—but that his stories varied, suggesting, as Dan Quayle argued during the vice-presidential debate, that "Bill Clinton has a problem telling the truth." It stirred fears among middle Americans that Clinton was too close to what they see as liberalism's moral flabbiness, too unwilling to offend, too prone to seek compromise, lacking any standard of justice except civil peace.[107]

The problem of guiding principles was exemplified in the debate over "family values." When they responded to Quayle, Russell Baker observed, liberals too often sounded "as though they're against love, marriage and family."[108] Unnecessarily so; recognizing that single-parent families face special difficulties does not entail rejection or ostracism but calls for appropriate assistance. Paradoxically, the liberal inclination to denounce as repressive any idea that the two-parent family is a standard leaves liberals only a limited, economic justification for aiding single-parent households, while conservatives, who accept the standard, are too niggardly to offer help.

Clinton avoided that ideological trap. He defused a good deal of the Republican appeal to "family values" by observing that, apart from restrictions on abortion and on gays, it was largely talk. And in his soft way, he was just as clear about the defects of liberalism: "Family values alone won't feed a hungry child, and material security can't provide a moral compass. We must have both."[109] Yet Clinton's shrewd claiming of the sensible middle ground left his family policy vague, like much of the agenda of the Clinton administration, still waiting to be defined.[110]

At the beginning of the campaign, the need for a moral compass led E.J. Dionne, Jr., to recommend the earlier, tougher liberalism symbolized by Humphrey Bogart in *Casablanca*.* To

---

*   E.J. Dionne, Jr., "Bogart in '92: The Fundamental Things Apply," his detriment, a great many voters could not shake the fear that Clinton might be something closer to Claude Rains's portrayal of a smooth, unprincipled opportunist. But in the end, Rains's policeman went off with Bogart's Rick to join the Free French, and there is reason to hope that Clinton will do at least as well.

As a campaigner, Clinton kept his coalition pretty much together, but the presidency will be a harder test. More or less united against Bush and the Reagan legacy, Democrats will be more apt to squabble when the question is what they are for.[111] Even during the campaign, many of Clinton's middle American supporters were bothered by the exclusion of Robert Casey, Pennsylvania's antiabortion governor, from a convention platform that had been opened to pro-choice Republican women.[112] It was an example of the abiding fear of middle American Democrats that liberals will be more at ease in the corridors of power and that, in a Clinton administration, the "new" Democratic Party will be swallowed by the "old." It will not help that some items high on the liberal agenda, including many aspects of abortion and gay rights, can be achieved fairly easily by executive order, while the hopes of middle Americans call for structural solutions, a long process of legislation and considerable pain.[113]

Judged by the campaign, Clinton can be expected to attend to such feelings and to the demand that burdens be shared fairly. But sacrifice, likely to be asked of all of us, will call for more than a gift for conciliation and the brokering of interests. It will demand a scale of justice and the conviction that our dignities and destinies are bound up with the common good.

Clinton shows every sign of concern to strengthen the government's title to rule and its claims on our allegiance. If he is wise, he will promote the use of public policy to rebuild the

---

Washington Post National Weekly, 16–22 December 1991, 25. Ironically, Dionne's own defense of the moral center in *Why Americans Hate Politics* (New York: Simon and Schuster, 1991) has been criticized by David O'Brien as "too easy and too conciliatory," *American Political Science Review* 86 (1992): 800.

links between citizens and their government, not simply media gimmicks, but local governments, parties, and associations with the "power of meeting," where citizens can learn the habits of democracy and the arts of politics.[114]

Yet ultimately, both in relation to his party and the country as a whole, Clinton's success will depend on his ability to articulate measures of public purpose and policy. For a Democrat, equality is the enduring grail, and in his best moments, Clinton's rhetoric of citizenship pointed to equality's vital contemporary meanings. Civic equality is no prescription for uniformity, not even in the form of enforced diversity. As Barbara Jordan told the Democratic convention, equality and equal rights are the conditions of civil variety. For Americans, their differing faiths and cultures are sources of strength, but no one needs to be told, these days, that cultures are not always easily compatible with each other or with democratic politics, that cultures often include racism and sexism, or that some nurture a hunger for dominion or are otherwise at odds with democratic life. America's version of multiculturalism accepts diversity, but only on the understanding that all cultures yield any claim to rule that runs counter to equality and equal rights. From an egalitarian point of view, cultures are not "separate realities" but more or less adequate answers to the human problem, to which equality and the rights that go with it are qualitatively superior because, unlike stories and legends, they rest on the stark truth of human nature.[115]

An excellent campaign slogan, "Putting People First," also hints at broader meanings, just as the reconciliation with nature to which Al Gore calls America implies more than our relation to the nonhuman environment. From its Columbian beginnings, America has been caught up in the modern quest for the mastery of nature, the rejection of whatever humans have not chosen or made. It becomes ever clearer, however, that technological mastery subordinates us to the things we have made and, left to itself, tends to dispense with human craft and devotion.* Yet

_____

* Raising the too-present danger, Albert Borgmann observes that the United States also began by asserting the proposition that both our equality and our rights are things that we did not make and about which we have no choice, an unalienable heritage from nature. If people are to come first in public policy, human nature must be given its due. Human beings are more than consumers, and their dignity—their need to be needed—deserves to be afforded at least equal status with the pursuit of abundance and mastery. Equality implies more than rights; it suggests that, within the limits of our circumstances, we can and should be held accountable to equal standards, offered and expected to live up to the opportunity to contribute to the common life. Even in speech, Bill Clinton's promise of a "new covenant" sounded chords of memory; it remains to be seen how far he can take Americans toward a rediscovery of the Republic.

Notes

1. "George Herbert Hoover Bush," *Economist,* 31 October 1992, 30.

2. David Broder, "Clinton's No Kennedy Either," *Washington Post National Weekly,* 12–18 October 1992, 4; Steven Greenhouse, "Clinton's Economic Plan Has a Roosevelt Tone," *New York Times,* 9 July 1992, 30.

3. David McCullough, *Truman* (New York: Simon and Schuster, 1992), 660–61, 668.

4. Russell Baker, "All Joy Departed," *New York Times,* 13 October 1992, A23.

5. R.W. Apple, Jr., "The Economy's Casualty," *New York Times,* 4 November 1992, A1.

6. *San Francisco Chronicle,* 20 August 1992, B3.

7. Robert D. Hershey, Jr., "The Politics of Declining Incomes," *New York Times,* 9 March 1992, D6.

the public will be reduced to sullen consumers on one hand and hyperactive careerists on the other. *Crossing the Postmodern Divide* (Chicago: University of Chicago Press, 1992).

8. Jim Hoagland, "Bush: First of Many to Fall," *Washington Post National Weekly,* 12–18 October 1992, 29.

9. Michael S. Lewis-Beck, *Economics and Elections* (Ann Arbor: University of Michigan Press, 1988); Michael MacKuen, Robert S. Erickson, and James A. Stimson, "Peasants or Bankers: The American Electorate and the U.S. Economy," *American Political Science Review* 86 (1992): 597–611; Donald Kinder and D. Roderick Kiewiet, "Economic Grievances and Political Behavior: The Role of Personal Discontents and Collective Judgments in Congressional Voting," *American Journal of Political Science* 23 (1979): 495–527.

10. Hobart Rowen, "Misdiagnosing the Recession," *Washington Post National Weekly,* 27 January–12 February 1992, 5.

11. David Broder, "The Uneasy Electorate," *Washington Post National Weekly,* 22–28 July 1991, 4; Leonard Silk, "The Many Faces of the Electorate," *New York Times,* 10 April 1992, D2.

12. *Notes on Virginia,* Letter to John Jay, 31 August 1785, and Letter to John Adams, 28 October 1813, all in Adrienne Koch and William Peden, eds., *The Life and Selected Writings of Jefferson* (New York: Modern Library, 1944), 280, 377, 633.

13. William Schmidt, "Hard Work Can't Stop Hard Times," *New York Times,* 25 November 1990, 1ff. For the best days of industrial labor, see E.E. LeMasters, *Blue Collar Aristocrats* (Madison: University of Wisconsin Press, 1975).

14. Frank Levy, *Dollars and Dreams* (New York: Russell Sage Foundation, 1987); Juliet Shor, *The Overworked American* (New York: Basic Books, 1991); Jodie T. Allen, "It's Morning in America, All Right," *Washington Post National Weekly,* 4–10 November 1991, 23.

15. Paul Starr, "The New Politics of Health Care," *Harper's,* October 1991, 22–30.

16. *New York Times,* 22 February 1992, L9. See also Sylvia Nasar, "The 1980s: A Very Good Time for the Very Rich," *New York Times,* 5 March 1992, 1ff.

17. Sylvia Nasar, "Fed Gives New Evidence of '80's Gains by Richest," *New York Times,* 21 April 1992, 1ff; Charles Murray, "The Shape of Things to Come," *National Review,* 8 July 1991, 29–30.

18. Robert Samuelson, "White Collar Blues," *Washington Post National Weekly,* 6–12 January 1992, 29.

19. Carl Rowan, "GOP Hasn't Been Kind to 'Family Values,'" *Star-Ledger,* 7 August 1992, 20; Steven Nock and P.W. Kingston, "Time with Children: The Impact of Couples' Work-Time Commitments," *So-*

cial Forces 67 (1988): 59–85.

20. Gerald M. Pomper, ed., *The Election of 1988* (Chatham, N.J.: Chatham House, 1989), 194–95; Mickey Kaus, *The End of Equality* (New York: Basic Books, 1992), 55–57; James Q. Wilson, "Crime, Race and Values," *Society,* December 1992, 90–93.

21. Robert Reich, "The Secession of the Successful," *New York Times Magazine,* 20 January 1991, 17ff; the term autoanesthesia is from Joseph Lyford's *The Airtight Cage* (New York: Harper, 1966).

22. Norman J. Ornstein, "Foreign Policy in the 1992 Elections," *Foreign Affairs* 71 (Summer 1992): 3, 7; Sidney Blumenthal saw that 1988 was the "last campaign of the Cold War": *Pledging Allegiance* (New York: HarperCollins, 1990).

23. Leslie Gelb, "No National Interest," *New York Times,* 18 October 1992, E15, and "Bush Gets Tough on Iraq," *New York Times,* 23 August 1992, E15.

24. Richard Morin, "How Quickly They Regret," *Washington Post National Weekly,* 20–26 January 1992, 37.

25. Jeffrey Frank, "Buy American or Bye, American," *Washington Post National Weekly,* 21–27 September 1992, 25; Lawrence Harrison, "Huddled Masses, Unskilled Labor," *Washington Post National Weekly,* 20–26 January 1992, 25.

26. Leslie Gelb, "Three Whine Mice," *New York Times,* 13 January 1992, A15.

27. Ibid.; on Clinton, see William Safire, "Bush-Clinton Debate," *New York Times,* 2 April 1992, A23.

28. Pomper, *The Election of 1988,* 189–90.

29. Hobart Rowen, "Productivity Not the Problem," *Washington Post National Weekly,* 30 November–5 December 1992, 5.

30. For example, see Daniel P. Moynihan, "A Landmark for Families," *New York Times,* 16 November 1992, A13.

31. Joel Garreau, "It's a Mall World After All," *Washington Post National Weekly,* 10–16 August 1992, 25.

32. Aristotle, *Ethics,* trans. J.A.K. Thompson (Harmondsworth, England: Penguin, 1956), book 2, chap. 1, pp. 55–56.

33. James Davison Hunter, *Culture Wars: The Struggle to Define America* (New York: Basic Books, 1991).

34. Tom Wicker, "An Alienated Public," *New York Times,* 13 October 1991, E15.

35. Humphrey Taylor, "The American Angst of 1992," *Public Perspective* 3 (July/August 1992): 3, table 1.

36. Rohde is cited by Dan Balz, "America the Morning After," *Washington Post National Weekly,* 21–27 October 1991, 13–14.

37. Jeffrey Schmalz, "Words on Bush's Lips in '88 Now Stick in Voters' Craw," *New York Times,* 14 June 1992, 1.

38. Martin P. Wattenberg, *The Decline of American Political Parties, 1952–1988* (Cambridge, Mass. : Harvard University Press, 1990).

39. Richard Zeiger, "Few Citizens Make Decisions for Everyone," *California Journal* 21 (November 1990): 517, 519; the belief in universal corruption is cited by Leslie Gelb, "Throw the Bums Out," *New York Times,* 23 October 1991, A23.

40. Garry Wills, "Ross Perot and the Immaculate Election," *Washington Post National Weekly,* 1–7 June 1992, 23; see also William Safire, "Protesting Too Much," *New York Times,* 6 April 1992, A19.

41. Richard Morin and E.J. Dionne, Jr., "Turning Down the Party Invitation," *Washington Post National Weekly,* 13–19 July 1992, 9; much the same position is espoused by Theodore Lowi, "The Party Crasher," *New York Times Magazine,* 23 August 1992, 28ff.

42. Anthony Lewis, "Time for a Change," *New York Times,* 9 April 1992, A25.

43. Russell Baker, "Potomac Breakdown," *New York Times,* 12 October 1991, 29; Lewis, "Time for a Change."

44. David Rosenbaum, "The Paralysis of No-Pain Politics," *New York Times,* 19 April 1992, E1; Roberto Suro, "Viewing Chaos in the Capital, Americans Express Outrage," *New York Times,* 19 November 1990, 1ff; Adam Clymer, "Citing Rise in Frustration, Dozens of Lawmakers Quit," *New York Times,* 5 April 1992, 1ff. On the Balanced Budget Amendment, see David Broder, "A Congressional Balancing Act," *Washington Post National Weekly,* 25–31 May 1992, 4.

45. James Q. Wilson, "The Newer Deal," *New Republic,* 2 July 1990, 34; Daniel Yankelovich, *Coming to Public Judgment* (Syracuse, N.Y.: Syracuse University Press, 1991), 4.

46. Jeffrey Schmalz, "Americans Sign Up in Record Numbers to Cast a Ballot," *New York Times,* 19 October 1992, 1ff; compare Paul R. Abramson and John H. Aldrich, "The Decline of Electoral Participation in America," *American Political Science Review* 76 (1982): 502–21.

47. Dan Balz, "They're Angry but Not Apathetic," *Washington Post National Weekly,* 26 October–1 November 1992, 13.

48. Tocqueville, *Democracy in America,* 1:210–11; 2:137.

49. Ibid., 2:134–37.

50. Bill Moyers, "The Old News and the New Civil War," *New*

York Times, 22 March 1992, E15.

51. Russell Baker, "Hear America Listening," *New York Times,* 2 November 1991, 23.

52. Wicker, "An Alienated Public."

53. Thomas Rosenstiel, "Networks Rethink Political Coverage," *Berkshire Eagle,* 17 July 1991, C6; Anthony Lewis, "Hair on their Chests," *New York Times,* 19 April 1992, E11; "Old News Deconstructed," *Economist,* 31 October 1992, 23.

54. *New York Times,* 11 July 1992, L7.

55. Todd Gitlin, "On Being Sound-Bitten," *Boston Review,* December 1991, 17.

56. Russell Baker, "You'd Hate It There," *New York Times,* 7 December 1991, 23; Roger Masters, Sigfried Frey, and Gary Bente, "Dominance and Attention: Images of Leaders in German, French and American TV News," *Polity* 23 (1991): 393.

57. John Tierney, "Now, Journalists Renege on Election Promises," *New York Times,* 31 January 1992, A12; newspaper coverage of TV ads similarly focused on strategy. Randall Rothenberg, "Newspapers Watch What People Watch in the TV Campaign," *New York Times,* 4 November 1990, E5.

58. Maureen Dowd, "Populist Media Forums and the Campaign of '92," *New York Times,* 3 November 1992, 14; Howard Kurtz, "The Year the Candidates Took to the Airwaves," *Washington Post National Weekly,* 2–8 November 1992, 14.

59. Elizabeth Kolbert, "Heard by Few, Clinton Speech Shows Candidates' Quandary," *New York Times,* 9 April 1992, A21.

60. Elizabeth Kolbert, "Perot Takes Issue while Clinton Takes on Issues," *New York Times,* 12 June 1992, A14.

61. Joe S. Foote, *Television Access and Political Power* (New York: Praeger, 1990).

62. Hume is cited by Richard Berke, "Campaign '92," *New York Times,* 26 June 1992, A13; Masters et al., "Dominance and Attention"; Jan Hoffman, "Larry King: Kingmaker to the Pols," *New York Times,* 28 June 1992, H27.

63. Gerald Marzorati, "From Tocqueville to Perotville," *New York Times,* 28 June 1992, E17.

64. David Broder, "Tabloid Election," *Washington Post National Weekly,* 3–9 February 1992, 4. The importance of local media in 1992 is a somewhat more hopeful sign. See Phyllis Kaniss, "A Victory for Local News," *New York Times,* 5 December 1992, 19.

65. Michael Paul Rogin, "JFK: The Movie," *American Historical Review* 97 (1992): 502, 505. Sidney Blumenthal saw many of the same themes in Jerry Brown's campaign. "He's a New Age Demagogue," *New York Times,* 5 April 1992, E17.

66. Rogin, "JFK," 503; Lloyd Grove, "Looking for President Perfect," *Washington Post National Weekly,* 6–12 April 1992, 6–7.

67. Steven Holmes, "Perot-Bush 'Dirty Tricks' Feud Persists," *New York Times,* 27 October 1992, A1ff; on Perot's dealings with Hanoi, see *New York Times,* 4 June 1992, 1.

68. Gwen Ifill, "Perot's Popularity Sends Clinton into Frustration," *New York Times,* 25 May 1992, 8; see also Elizabeth Kolbert's report on Perot's spending, *New York Times,* 28 October 1992, A1.

69. Walter Goodman, "Perot Leaves a Field of Broken Rules," *New York Times,* 10 October 1992, 46.

70. Maureen Dowd, "Once Again, Questions of Character," *New York Times,* 28 June 1992, E1.

71. David Broder, "A Knight in Shining Armor," *Washington Post National Weekly,* 4–10 May 1992, 4; Peter Milius, "Ross Perot's Fuzz," *Washington Post National Weekly,* 11–17 May 1992, 29.

72. John Mintz and David Von Drehle, "The Day Perot Pulled the Plug," *Washington Post National Weekly,* 27 July–2 August 1992, 9.

73. Perot's style should be compared to Richard Rosenstone's observations in "Historical Fact / Historical Film," *American Historical Review* 97 (1992): 507.

74. Dan Balz and E.J. Dionne, Jr., "In a Quirky Year, Perot Could Be a Loose Cannon," *Washington Post National Weekly,* 4–10 May 1992, 8.

75. Wills, "Ross Perot and the Immaculate Election"; Michael Kelly, "Perot's Vision: Consensus by Computer," *New York Times,* 6 June 1922, 1ff; Richard Cohen, "Deconstructing Perot," *Washington Post National Weekly,* 18–24 May 1992, 28.

76. Michael Schrage, "Perot: A Man of Revolution, Not Evolution," *Washington Post,* 1 May 1992, B3; Steven Greenhouse, "Hardly Laissez-Faire," *New York Times,* 27 June 1992, L9.

77. Kevin Sack, "Why Perot Thrived in Fertile Kansas," *New York Times,* 6 November 1992, A20.

78. Hicks, *Populist Revolt,* 234.

79. Thomas Byrne Edsall, "Those Crucial Voters Not Yet Heard From," *Washington Post National Weekly,* 30 March–5 April 1992, 12; my comments on the Buchanan vote derive from *New York Times* exit

polls (e.g., 5 March 1992, A22).

80. *New York Times,* 5 March 1992, A22, for Clinton's vote on Super Tuesday. In New York, Tsongas—no longer an active candidate—had an edge among white Christians. Clinton depended on his margin among blacks and Jews. *New York Times,* 9 April 1992, A20.

81. Thomas Byrne Edsall with Mary D. Edsall, *Chain Reaction: The Impact of Race, Rights and Taxes on American Politics* (New York: Norton, 1992); Ronald P. Formisano, *Boston Against Busing* (Chapel Hill: University of North Carolina Press, 1991), 232–33.

82. The comments of Robert Huckfeldt and Carol Weitzel Kohfeld are apposite. See *Race and the Decline of Class in American Politics* (Champaign: University of Illinois Press, 1989), ix, 188.

83. David Broder, "Jackson's Decline, Brown's Ascent," *Washington Post National Weekly,* 20–26 July 1992, 4.

84. Ronald Brownstein, "New Studies of U.S. Tensions Put Focus on Class, Not Race," *Berkshire Eagle,* 28 July 1991, A3; William Julius Wilson, *The Truly Disadvantaged* (Chicago: University of Chicago Press, 1987).

85. Lena Williams, "In a 90s' Quest for Black Identity, Intense Doubts and Disagreement," *New York Times,* 30 November 1991, 1ff.

86. William Julius Wilson, "The Right Message," *New York Times,* 17 March 1992, A25.

87. Orlando Patterson, "Our History vs. Clinton's Covenant," *New York Times,* 13 November 1992.

88. John J. Farmer, "Republicans Sound Like the Ideologues Now," *Star-Ledger,* 13 August 1992, 24; Garry Wills, "George Bush: Prisoner of the Crazies," *New York Times,* 16 August 1992, E17.

89. *New York Times,* 5 November 1992, B9.

90. Andrew Rosenthal, "The Politics of Morality," *New York Times,* 22 May 1992, A19; on the Republican campaign, see Robin Toner, "How Bush Lost Five Chances to Save the Day," *New York Times,* 11 October 1992, E1ff.

91. Harvey Mansfield, *America's Constitutional Soul* (Baltimore: Johns Hopkins University Press, 1991), 69.

92. David Rosenbaum, "Missing from Politics: The Blueprints for the Future," *New York Times,* 2 February 1992, E1; Blumenthal, *Pledging Allegiance,* 49–76.

93. "President Noodle," *New York Times,* 5 March 1992, A26; George Will, "Serious People Flinch," *Washington Post National Weekly,* 31 August–6 September 1992, 29.

94. Mary McGrory, "You Say Potato and I Say It Takes Only 35 Percent to Win," *Washington Post National Weekly,* 29 June–5 July 1992, 25; Kevin Phillips, "GOP Crackup," *New York Times,* 4 June 1992, A23.

95. John Green and James Guth, "The Christian Right in the Republican Party," *Journal of Politics* 50 (1988): 150–65.

96. David Maraniss, "Clinton's Journey of the Spirit," *Washington Post National Weekly,* 13–19 July 1992, 10–11.

97. The figures are 23 percent and 18 percent respectively. *New York Times,* 5 November 1992, B9.

98. Garry Wills, "The Hostage," *New York Review of Books,* 13 August 1992, 21–27.

99. Thomas Byrne Edsall, "The GOP May Be Losing Its Realignment Linchpin," *Washington Post National Weekly,* 21–27 September 1992, 15; Mary Jordan, "More Freshmen Lean to Left," *Washington Post National Weekly,* 20–26 January 1992, 37.

100. Clinton drew 44 percent of voters aged 18–29. Dukakis had attracted 47 percent. *New York Times,* 5 November 1992, B9; Barbara Vobejda, "Family Value Voting," *Washington Post National Weekly,* 30 November–5 December 1992, 36.

101. Peter Cellupica, "The Political Dawn Arrives for Gays," *New York Times,* 7 November 1992, 21; David Broder argues that homophobia among Republicans and from Perot, by guaranteeing that Jackson's gay financial backers had no alternative, helped encourage Clinton to criticize Sister Souljah. Broder, "Jackson's Decline, Brown's Ascent."

102. Harvey Schantz, "The Erosion of Sectionalism in American Elections" *Polity* 24 (1992): 355–77.

103. Robin Toner, "Clinton's Southern Roots Trip Him in New York," *New York Times,* 1 April 1992, A20.

104. Meredith Nicholson, *The Valley of Democracy* (New York: Scribners, 1918).

105. Mary Ann Glendon, *Rights Talk: The Impoverishment of Political Discourse* (New York: Basic Books, 1991).

106. The Democrats' internal conflict is well presented by David Carlin, "Blame the Message," *Commonweal,* 8 May 1992, 9–10; and Margaret O'Brien Steinfels, "Safe, Legal and Rare," *Commonweal,* 20 November 1992, 4–5.

107. This critique of liberalism was the message of Ben Wattenberg's PBS special on the Democrats. (See Walter Goodman's review, *New York Times,* 16 October 1992, B16.) Clinton's record provides

some support for his critics: David Maraniss, "Clinton's Arkansas Legacy," *Washington Post National Weekly,* 26 October–1 November 1992, 7.

108. Russell Baker, "To Cloud Men's Minds," *New York Times,* 23 May 1992.

109. Gwen Ifill, "Clinton Sees Bush Engaging in Empty Talk on Families," *New York Times,* 22 May 1992, A18.

110. For a realistic "family agenda," see Timothy Bates, "Paying for Values: The Real Needs of Real Families," *Commonweal,* 9 October 1992, 6–7.

111. Thomas Byrne Edsall, "Nibbling Rivalry: Democrats Are One Big, Scrappy Family," *Washington Post National Weekly,* 16–22 November 1992, 23.

112. Walter Goodman, "The Convention Images: Plenty for Both Sides," *New York Times,* 18 July 1992, 49.

113. David Rosenbaum, "No Painless Way Out for the Next President," *New York Times,* 4 October 1992, E1.

114. Tocqueville, *Democracy in America,* 1:217–18; 2:124.

115. Bill Moyers, "Old News and the New Civil War."

7

Slouching toward the Millennium:
The Election of 1994

It looked as if a night of dark intent
Was coming. And not only a night, an age.
Someone had better be prepared for rage.

—Robert Frost, "Once by the Pacific"

Summer 1994 (19 August 1994)

Politically, this is a summer of discontents. Most Americans seem irritated by politics; Congressman Bill Richardson (D-New Mexico) called the public mood "antsy"—impatient with leaders but too listless to follow. The electorate is not angry, the usual frothing ideologues aside, so much as disappointed in government and at least half disposed to give up on public life. The hesitant hopefulness that surfaced in 1992 has pretty much vanished, and Americans appear to be looking, often despairingly, to their private defenses.

It is not just Bill Clinton, although unhappiness with the president is a big part of the story. In California, despite prolonged hard times and sharply contested races between interesting candidates in both parties, turnout in the June primary was the lowest in the state's history—38 percent of registered voters—and the electorate turned down every proposal to issue bonds for public improvement.[1] And from Senator George

Mitchell (D-Maine) down, elected officials in droves are returning to private life, finding the satisfactions of a career in democratic politics no longer worth the costs.

For the Democrats, this makes grim news, especially since
in an off-year election, running against a president with less
than rousing approval ratings, Republicans already could expect
to make significant gains. An important part of the Democratic
edge in congressional and local elections has derived from the
party's greater ability to attract "quality" candidates, and when
the allure of politics wanes, Democrats are bound to be losers. It
is even more important that lower-income, nonwhite, and hence
likely Democratic voters are disproportionately staying home.
The more citizens need government, after all, the more apt they
are to feel resentful when it falls short, so it is not entirely para-
doxical that in one 1993 survey, 53 percent of Republicans, but
only 40 percent of Democrats, were willing to say that government generally is beneficial to the people.[2]

As it stands, Democrats will be lucky to hold their losses to
two or three seats in the Senate and twenty in the House, and as
every major vote tells us, the president has none to spare. In the
gubernatorial races, Mario Cuomo (D-New York) is a good bet
for reelection, but Ann Richards (D-Texas) is at least worried; in
California, Kathleen Brown, who once looked like an easy winner, may even trail the Republican incumbent, Pete Wilson,
while Senator Dianne Feinstein, a Democrat, also once far
ahead, faces a real, and very expensive, campaign.

For Bill Clinton and his party, the immediate political problem is the need to reanimate their friends and well-wishers; the
president's enemies may even be a help. Clinton probably could
have ignored the radio right-wingers, knaves though they are.
Those voters who supported—and most of those who might
ever support—Clinton and the Democrats almost certainly are
disinclined to accept the more lurid versions of Whitewater,
l'affaire Jones, and the like, and they are showing some recognition that such matters, at most, are largely irrelevant to Clinton's presidency. In any event, those stories, for the moment, are

not commanding television headlines, and what is off-screen, for the American public, tends to go quickly out of mind.

By contrast, Clinton does need to worry about the wholly relevant and troubling questions about his *public* character. As a political leader, Bill Clinton sounds a very uncertain saxophone. With alarming consistency, the president stakes out a strong position and then backs off, or backs down, when confronted by opposition or new information. This is most obvious in foreign policy, but it began with the question of gays in the military, the administration's entree, and it has been just as visible in relation to Clinton's high-profile appointments or in policy issues such as the BTU tax. In part, this reflects the president's virtues: he learns, is willing to cut his losses, and in general ends with a sensible result. But unmistakably Bill Clinton suffers from his own problems with the "vision thing," a pragmatic focus on the best deal at the expense of moral leadership and civic education. Franklin Roosevelt, that foxy lion, sometimes followed a pattern like Clinton's—for example, in his retreat from the high ground of the Quarantine Speech—but as a rule, FDR kept his compromises off-stage, and he never forgot the political value of a strong line.[3] President Clinton's too-public improvisations, even when agile, have created an impression of moral weakness, making the friendliest voters worry that however skilled at keeping the ship afloat, Clinton has no clear sense of direction.

To be fair, some of the Clinton administration's shortcomings are institutional rather than personal. Our image of the presidency was framed by Roosevelt and his immediate successors, but it does Clinton an injustice to compare him to presidents past, and, Watergate and the like aside, even Nixon may be too high a mark.* We live in the era of a postmodern presidency, in which chief executives are dealt a much weaker hand. Congress is more intractable, fragmented by various "reforms,"

---

* William Leuchtenberg, *In the Shadow of FDR* (Ithaca, N.Y.: Cornell University Press, 1983); see Stephen Skowronek's perceptive anticipations regarding Clinton's presidency in *The Politics Presidents Make* (Cambridge, Mass.: Harvard University Press, 1993), 442–46.

its leadership weaker, its members less tied to presidential coat-tails and less susceptible to the appeals of party or patronage. In fact, what passes for good government nowadays makes it harder for a president to grease the legislative wheels with pol-icy favors and campaign support, or even to protect an ally like Dan Rostenkowski (D-Illinois).[4] To make matters worse, our growing dependence on the international economy means that the government cannot really claim mastery of its own house, and presidents cannot afford to be high-handed, especially now that world politics lacks the old disciplines of the Cold War. No one needs to be told, moreover, that the media are more intru-sive and adversarial, servants of a baffled and disorganized pub-lic whose distrust of authority and disinclination to sacrifice are a near balance to any desire for change. And, as Clinton himself demonstrates, what helps elect a postmodern president—being a credible voice for outsiders—is at odds with the qualities a pres-ident needs to govern.

Even so, Clinton's record after eighteen months in office is vastly more impressive than Kennedy's. Very few of Clinton's achievements, however, sing in Democratic ears or inspire popu-lar hosannas. Clinton's budget was our first serious encounter with the deficit, and it made a start at spreading the burden more fairly. But while most voters seem to have accepted the ne-cessity for Clinton's measures—there is no real public outcry, even among Republicans, against Clinton's taxes—they do not regard them as a reason for joy. The North American Free Trade Agreement (NAFTA), a major legislative victory for the administration, probably offended more Democrats than ad-mired it, and the reform of health care is still only a complicated and confusing possibility (though a crucial one for Clinton, since the overwhelming majority of his supporters, back in 1993, expected him to make progress on that front).

But above all, a Democratic administration is supposed to mean jobs, and the economic recovery, which should be the ad-ministration's strong point, has been both carefully moderated —a sensible policy, but not a popular one—and uneven. "Winner-take-all economics," as Robert Frank and Philip Cook call it, still looks like the rule.[5] It was clear a year ago that only a fraction of laid off workers were getting their old jobs back (14 percent, as against 44 percent in the past four recessions), and new layoffs and plant closings are stimulating a pervasive anxiety about work and the future, against which Robert Reich's emphasis on "counseling and retraining" sounds pretty feeble.[6] Clinton does not deserve all, or even much, of the blame; Ronald Reagan's profligacy took away much of our autonomy in policy and, even more, the president's freedom to maneuver. The United States has to satisfy its creditors; the international bond market calls most of the tunes; there never seems to be any money for public programs.[7]

Yet Democratic constituencies, facing need and fear, are not inclined to be understanding. A considerable number of Clinton's critics on the liberal left worry that the president is too inclined to defer to orthodox economics and too willing to make economic "growth," whatever the social cost, the standard of public policy. This November, Clinton and the Democrats had better have an answer to such charges, and not in words alone.[8]

Still, the president and his party have some major assets. Bill Clinton has neutralized much of the old conservative advantage on social issues, one reason why the right hates him so luxuriantly. Democrats have been taking a tough stance toward crime, even if a lot of it has been posturing, and the president has made welfare reform a respectable, even mandatory, part of any Democratic platform.[9] Of course, abortion and gun control are intensely controversial, and the president's compromises on gay rights have irritated the left without conciliating the right; but on all these issues, opinion probably leans to the Democratic side. And while it generates rumbling in the Black Caucus and on the street, the administration so far has kept race off the political center stage.

These aspects of Clinton's New Democracy have stopped or reversed Republican gains in the two-party balance: younger voters are tilting away from what had been Republican leanings, and, recently, voters have been rating Democrats equal to Republicans in their ability to deal with crime and the deficit and superior in relation to health care, welfare reform, and, despite everything, unemployment. They may resent Clinton's stumblings and vacillations in foreign policy, but they admire the fact that the country is at peace and regard Democrats as a better bet to preserve it. The shadow in this sunshine, for the Democrats, is that voters see Republicans, the recent recession to the contrary, as more likely to produce economic prosperity.[10] And that may tip the scales decisively in 1994.

Anyone who occupies the White House, however, holds a good many trumps, and Clinton shows signs of trying to address doubts about his leadership. His choice of Leon Panetta as chief of staff is more than reassuring, and it has the side benefit of elevating Alice Rivlin, that nonpareil, to first place in the Office of Management and Budget. There may even be stirrings in foreign policy. At the Naples economic summit, for example, the president refused to panic over the decline in the value of the dollar, trusting in the "fundamentals" of the U.S. recovery, a defiance of currency traders that even the New York Times, not always admiring, called "gutsy."

But it would really be a political masterstroke if Clinton found a new secretary of state. Warren Christopher has his moments—as he did last year, when he told the world Conference on Human Rights that we "cannot let cultural relativism become the last refuge of repression" at the expense of universal standards—but, at bottom, he is only another lawyerly negotiator, not the strong political voice the president needs.* Were he replaced by a Walter Mondale or a Colin Powell, it would set bells ringing, here and abroad.

Above all, the president needs to do something that is visibly strong, that shows him to have courage and conviction as

---

* For Christopher's criticism of cultural relativism, see New York Times, 15 June 1993, A1. Maureen Dowd commented, early in the Clinton administration, on the president's penchant for lawyerly advisors. "Washington Memo," New York Times, 13 February 1993, A8.

well as cunning, as his rebuke to Sister Souljah did in 1992. A showy success in foreign policy would help, but the president is too decent to go looking for a Grenada. He may get his chance on health care; his vow to veto any bill that lacks universal, irrevocable coverage was too unambiguous to be explained away, and if Congress flinches, it will be up to Clinton to stand the fire.

In any event, Democrats are always at their worst when talking to each other. Every element of the crazy-quilt Democratic coalition has reason to be annoyed with the Clinton administration, and none has shown much reluctance to say so. But the closer they get to Republicans, the more Democrats are inspired to a simulacrum of civility. So far in 1994, mainstream Republicans virtually have no policies, at least none that they feel comfortable advocating in public. Senator Bob Dole's (R-Kansas) cleaving to the line of pure opposition will not be sufficient in an election, since citizens expect to hear something like answers, and reliance on the market, the Republican lodestar, plays very uncertainly with working- and middle-class voters, who suspect that the costs of that policy fall hardest on them.[11]

In fact, the absence of an articulated alternative from mainstream Republicans has strengthened the only-too-verbal legions of the right, religious and otherwise, whose intraparty victories have been very much in the media, much to the Democrats' delight. Senator Charles Robb (D-Virginia) would be a dead duck against anyone but Oliver North (although that race will turn on which of the two independent candidates, Douglas Wilder or Marshall Coleman, eventually proves to have more supporters who cannot bear to waste their votes). With wonderful irony, Congressman Vic Fazio (D-California) called the religious right a "godsend" to the Democrats, and perhaps it is, since nothing is more likely to move the party's faithful and drive moderates into its arms.[12]

Democrats have reason to feel queasy, but, Republican follies aside, they know that whatever his weaknesses in governing, President Clinton is no slouch at campaigning. It is a long time until November, and the Cleveland Indians, barring a baseball strike, are a real contender in their division. Strange and wonderful things may yet happen in 1994.

The Storm Ahead (21 October 1994)

Maybe along with the World Series we ought to cancel the elections on 8 November. The Democrats, sure losers, wouldn't complain; even the confident Republicans have problems. But it is the Republic that may have the greatest troubles of all.

The citizenry might as well be on strike. Turnout will be low, a mortal hurt for Democrats. Bill Clinton has many excellences, but neither his pragmatism nor his conciliatory instincts rally the multitudes, and his policies have not offered a battle cry.[13] The electorate will be disproportionately white and upper income, overrepresenting the kind of voters who lean Republican and care about such issues as crime, a major theme for the Bush boys, George and Jeb, in their gubernatorial campaigns in Texas and Florida, and for more substantial candidates elsewhere.

Gloomy all summer, the Democratic mood suffered from the crime bill's stumble to passage and from the failure to deliver on health care; so far, things are no better than they were in August and probably a little worse. Democrats can now expect to lose at least four seats in the Senate (including two, in Maine and Ohio, that they had reason to count on) and something like twenty to twenty-five in the House. Thanks to Douglas Wilder's withdrawal, Senator Charles Robb should beat Oliver North in Virginia, but it is not a sure thing; Ann Richards has a nominal edge for governor of Texas, but Kathleen Brown is fighting uphill in California, and Mario Cuomo is trailing in New York.

Such good tidings as the Democrats have received recently have come mostly from foreign policy, despite Clinton's established reputation for bumbling improvisation. (Actually, here as in many things, the president's record is better than his press; the administration has a number of successes—in the Middle East, the Baltic States, and Northern Ireland—that discretion forbids it to trumpet too loudly.)[14] In Haiti, after a half-dozen false starts, Clinton showed strength enough to order the invasion despite the polls, and wound up with a deal that, problematic as it is, lets him curb the junta without overcommitment to Aristide. The relatively peaceful occupation gave the president's ratings a small, temporary lift. And Clinton's Republican opponents wound up sounding like isolationists and wrong in the bargain.

Confrontations with Caribbean dictators, in fact, may be the president's best suit. His handling of the latest Cuban refugee crisis was remarkably smooth and paid political dividends: Jorge Mas Canosa, that titan among Cuban conservatives, compared Clinton favorably to Reagan and Bush as a champion of "democracy and freedom" who had "stood up" to Castro, and Florida's Governor Lawton Chiles, the recipient of equally lavish praise, has become one of the least terrified Democratic incumbents.[15]

In his policies toward Cuba and Haiti, moreover, Clinton understood that the desire to avoid massive immigration was his best lever on the electorate. And in both instances, a great many observers were pleased to see Secretary of State Warren Christopher relegated to the sidelines. In Haiti, Jimmy Carter got most of the headlines, but the political portent was Colin Powell's presence on the negotiating team, another of those carefully ambiguous intimations from the general that have been giving Republican strategists the sweats. But although Democrats will take what comfort they can, they know that such events are light airs at best, no change in the prevailing wind.

Not that the news is wholly rosy for the Republicans, although they are enjoying their prospective gains and the outside chance of taking one or both houses of Congress. Already, more voters blame the GOP for any gridlock in Washington than fault Clinton (by a margin of 48–32 percent).[16] And things will get worse; the Republicans are relying on a vote against Clinton, but the closer they get to power, the more they will find themselves under scrutiny. Up to this point, the media have been generous: Bill Clinton does vacillate, for example, but seldom so dramatically as Phil Gramm did on the crime bill, which he described (in November 1993) as the "toughest crime bill ever passed," only to tell us (in August 1994) that it coddles criminals.[17] There is also nothing like a positive Republican program. The closest approach, the "Contract with America" floated by House Republicans, was Reagan *redux* but without the master's charm: a balanced budget amendment, combined with massive tax cuts that supposedly will pay for themselves. The greater the chances for victory, the more people will balk at this sort of farrago: as George Pataki rose in the polls against New York's Governor Cuomo, the vagueness of Pataki's proposals attracted criticism from the left of his own party (New York Mayor Rudolph Giuliani), but also from its right (Herbert London, the candidate for state controller).

Far from turning to the Republicans, the electorate is becoming "unanchored": in one poll, no more than 29 percent of voters expressed an inclination to vote for a Democrat for Congress, but only 23 percent named Republicans. Almost half the electorate is in play; Virginia shows that independents and third parties are still likely to be squeezed out, but here and there (in Maine and Connecticut, for example), centrist third parties are serious contenders. Incumbents face an extraordinary discontent—an advantage for Republicans, in their role as outsiders *ex officio,* but only until they win. *All* our institutions—the parties, the Congress, the presidency, even the Constitution—are under challenge: 91 percent of voters told a *Time*/CNN poll that they had little or no confidence in government's ability to solve problems. Yet contrary to what Republicans might hope, this did not amount to an endorsement of the night watchman state; 90 percent also expressed a desire for "change"—for most, a demand for some sort of governmental activism—even though they did not agree about what should be changed or who should bear the cost. Too many voters, after weighing the disharmonies of democratic politics and the restraints of constitutionalism, are finding them wanting.[18]

Part of the problem is that our leaders in Congress (and elsewhere) have grown too accustomed to going their own way, too reluctant to accept the discipline and responsibility of party. Norman Ornstein is right to urge a cultivation of "followership"; even William Safire has found some kind words for loyalty, and a dose of civility would not hurt at all. And that goes for the rest of us. When we judge leaders, we are prone to get it wrong—public opinion to the contrary, Ornstein observes, most members of Congress are not moved "primarily or even significantly" by the desire for more money—and worse, we are apt to miss the moral point.[19] Private citizens tend to think of morality in private terms, principally in relation to avarice and sexual desire; they do not face, and hence may not recognize, the temptations of power, or that distinctive sin of democratic politicians, the craving for public love and favor. Local politics, the world of face-to-face parties and associations, used to offer a basic education in political morality through the curriculum of practice. The mass media, by contrast, speak to us in private places and appeal to private sentiments; they encourage our tendency to ask the wrong questions and arrive at the wrong answers. And the saddest part of contemporary elections, including this year's, is that everyone knows the media are a central part of the political problem—we hear complaints all the time—but there are no serious proposals for reforming the role of the media in public life.[20]

At least the economy is doing just fine, or so the experts say. Economists and corporate leaders, for the most part, cannot see anything to worry about except the trade deficit and the possibility that some whiff of inflation will lead the Federal Reserve to raise interest rates yet again. Jobs are being created at a faster rate than expected and at a relatively high level of quality, or so some studies argue. Any other result would mean total disaster for Clinton and the Democrats, elected in 1992 on the promise of prosperity.

But the economic expansion is not doing the Democrats much good. David Carlin is right that well-being on the economic front only allows Americans to worry about other issues such as the generally sorry state of the culture.[21] And as immediate fears recede for the comparatively prosperous, they are less apt to see economic difficulties as a common problem and more likely to regard them as something experienced by largely undeserving others. At the same time, their own long-term economic anxieties haunt them; they recognize that the deficit has only been dented, and their conviction that good jobs are hard to come by—the result of twenty years of decline in real wages, buttressed by continuing corporate white-collar layoffs and celebrations of "leanness"—is not about to be changed by a blip in labor statistics. They experience prosperity as a momentary relief rather than the rebirth of the American Dream.[22] In middle America, the mood is self-protective and ungenerous; since 1992, there has been a sharp fall in the percentage of Americans supporting aid to the needy. All in all, it is not surprising that in California, the major political beneficiary of Clinton-era job growth has been Republican Governor Pete Wilson, who has emphasized the strain on education and social services resulting from illegal immigration.

Health care, I suspect, has been another casualty of economic recovery. Something like 80 percent of Americans say they favor universal coverage, but any specific plan—and even more, any scheme for paying for one—loses supporters. And as middle-class Americans have grown less anxious about losing their own coverage, their concern to protect existing plans has waxed, while their enthusiasm for reform has waned. It is even a good guess that the mostly Democratic supporters of reform were not entirely unhappy with the failure to pass a bill: they can now run in favor of health care in whatever form seems likely to please their constituents, unencumbered by specific legislation. A comprehensive health bill was bound to be complicated and confusing; the Clinton plan, going beyond that necessity, amounted to Cambodian variations on the Byzantine, and

the quest for a congressional majority added to its own curli-
cues. The whole issue eventually made voters feel baffled, resentful, and inclined to play it safe, epitomizing the state of citizenship in contemporary America.

A growing number of Americans feel vulnerable and jerked
around by experts and interests, dominations and powers. And
more and more citizens are troubled by the moral and social
fragmentation of American life. They know, as Carlin suggests,
that we need to fix the foundations of our public house. It's no
accident that both the president and Dan Quayle have been
thumping the "family values" tub again.

But very few Americans are willing pay the price of addressing these concerns in more than peripheral ways. Any effort to strengthen family or community in America runs up
against deeply entrenched parts of our life: the two-wage-earner,
two-generation household; personal mobility; the "information
revolution"; the diminution of democratic politics in favor of
proliferating "rights." Conservatives are unwilling to interfere
with the individualizing logic of the economy; liberals are reluctant to constrain, or even to judge, freedom in "lifestyle." Both
sides find it easier to rest with the effort to persuade Americans
to uphold the decencies against the pressures and temptations of
the time. Yet even the way we talk reflects the problems we
hope speech will help us solve: "values" are preferences, not
ways of living, opinions only a little less mutable than the market. Values are not virtues any more than rights are equivalent
to righteousness, but the latter terms are indispensable to genuine reconstruction. If American culture is in fact the real issue in
1994, we seem a long way from recognizing the depth of its crisis.

Aftershock: Can Republicans Govern?
(2 December 1994)

Even a Jeremiah might have found the elections of 1994 a bit
much. There were scattered consolations: some Republican new-

comers, like Olympia Snowe in Maine, have real quality; Dianne Feinstein beat Michael Huffington; above all, as Democrats everywhere reminded each other, Oliver North lost in Virginia. But even Chicago voters, who used to know better, turned away from Dan Rostenkowski, and too many first-rate public servants, such as David Price in North Carolina, were rewarded with defeat.*

Voting was a tad higher than expected, about 39 percent of those eligible, and Republicans got more of their supporters to the polls. Differences in turnout certainly defeated Mario Cuomo, for example; 69 percent of upstate registered voters, but only 46 percent of those in New York City made it to the voting booth.[23] Resentment was the order of the day, at least among the part of the electorate that tipped the scales. Democrats, the targets of anger, also suffered from the disappointment and indifference of many potential supporters, and the one clear verdict in 1994 was against the party's stewardship since President Bill Clinton took office.

Beyond this negative message, the electorate's voice was inarticulate or incoherent. The voters chose divided government as a remedy for unproductive government and effectively asked for more ideological posturing, although that is probably the last thing they had in mind. "I do not know where they are going," former Republican senator Howard Baker said sensibly, "and I don't think they know where either. But . . . if we do not address their feelings, they may develop a tendency to savage our institutions." † Over the next two years, the Republican majorities in Congress will jockey for position against Clinton and the Democrats in the hope of turning this year's gain into a perma-

---

* Russell Baker recognized that Rostenkowski's public virtues and services deserve to outweigh offenses that—even presuming his guilt —are essentially venial. "Good Man on a Bad Scene," *New York Times*, 18 June 1994, 21.

† *New York Times*, 10 November 1994, B4. Thomas Mann called attention to the contradiction to the demand for change and the effective vote for increased ideological polarity. *USA Today*, 9 November 1994, 2A.

nent majority. The election of 1994, however, is more mood than mandate, and the political future is uncomfortably up for grabs.

Issues played a remarkably minor role in the election; upward of 70 percent of the voters, the polls tell us, have never even heard of the Republicans' "Contract with America." A very high percentage of the citizenry holds that government does not work and cannot be trusted, but this hostility, especially toward Washington, does not bespeak any particular confidence in market forces or the dynamics of private life.[24]

Americans think that something is fundamentally wrong with the economy, all the good numbers to the contrary; the Clinton administration's happy talk about those statistics only made it seem out of touch. For a long time, most Americans have been working more and getting less. Quality jobs are scarce, and some 25 percent of us expect a relative or close friend to become unemployed over the next few years. International competition is a constant threat, while pell-mell we are being asked to reshape ourselves to the measure of half-mysterious technologies. Immigration, an issue that helped reelect Republican Governor Pete Wilson in California and Democrat Lawton Chiles in Florida, typifies the more general truth that Americans, as Michael Sandel observes, are "haunted by the fear that we are losing control of the forces that govern our lives." *

The voters indicated some willingness to try Republican policies, particularly as a check-and-balance to Clinton's, but Republicans will get it wrong if they read the returns as an endorsement of laissez-faire.† GOP ideologues such as Bill Archer of Texas cherish dreams of doing away with the income tax, but the same Montana electorate that sent Republican Conrad Burns back to the Senate also rejected a proposal to limit the

---

* Michael Sandel's comments are taken from the *New York Times,* 10 November 1994, B5. For the impact of immigration on the elections in Florida and California, see ibid., B11–12.

† William Raspberry made this point in a post-election commentary, "It Doesn't Work," *Washington Post National Weekly,* 28 November–4 December 1994, 28.

state's graduated income tax. Voters expect government to be responsible for the economic and social future, and they cast their votes, above all, for policies that can reduce their sense of vulnerability.

Similarly, the voters' desire for effective measures against crime or to strengthen families point toward government and not away from it. Both parties will certainly advocate and try to take credit for some form of welfare reform, but insistence on "workfare," for example, entails providing the work as well as the day care and other services needed to make it feasible.

A good deal of the turn to the right in 1994 is also a rebuke to relativism and cultural elites. To that extent, Newt Gingrich is right: the results of the election are an affirmation of the decencies that Democrats will ignore at their peril. But Gingrich and his allies will have to take care not to overplay their hand; the decencies, for most Americans, include broad tolerance, and the voters in Idaho, sweeping the Democrats out of the state-house, also appear to have rejected a measure limiting gay rights. And attending to the malaise of the culture presumes a government with considerable responsibility for the reconstruction of the moral order.

For Democrats, 1994 should be a "call to arms," just as Doris Kearns says, but they will need a clearer recognition of their real strengths and weaknesses.[25] This year, Democrats lost across the electorate, Jews and African Americans excepted. The falling off was serious among men, but Democrats also lost some support from women, and Hispanic defections were notable. Yet the Democrats did not lose ground to the Republicans as a party; the balance of party preferences remained about even. And Democrats did relatively well with younger voters, confirming a shift away from the trend of the Reagan years.*

As I read the data, Republican gains in middle America of-

---

* *New York Times,* 10 November 1994, B7. Richard Berke, among many, made the argument that white male defections were crucial. "Defections Among Men to GOP Helped Insure Rout of Democrats," *New York Times,* 11 November 1994, A1.

fer the best explanation for the debacle of 1994.* Democrats suffered major losses among voters at middle levels of age, education, and income; Dianne Feinstein led Huffington among voters at the bottom, but also the top of the income scale. President Clinton's policies, the crime bill partially excepted, have not done much to address the concerns of middle Americans directly. Even his reduction in the deficit was successfully distorted by Republicans, so most Americans believe that the deficit has increased. And by championing NAFTA, Clinton allied himself, however wisely, with forces threatening the social world of middle America. Since Clinton's neoliberalism plays down any appeal to class conflict and cultivates corporate support, it is not entirely surprising, though it is certainly arresting, that half of the respondents in one poll identified the Democrats as the party of "the rich."[26] And such perceptions are magnified by the belief that Clinton's vacillations, his verbal affirmations to the contrary, reflect the relativist-to-nihilist strain of the cultural elite. Bill Clinton, to a substantial number of Americans, is less a boy from Hope than a man from Yale.

Historically, the Democrats have been the American party of equality, devoted to the belief that the majority has the right, within the limits of nature, to control its own political destiny. In recent years, however, the party has often seemed less interested in upholding majority rule than in limiting it in favor of the rights of minorities and other favored constituencies—no different, in this respect, from Republicans, the apologists for the rights of property. Both parties, in this sense, have developed an elitist strain, which explains why so many Americans are attracted by the doomed allure of a possible third party. After 1994, the Democrats have compelling reasons to reaffirm their commitment to what Chesterton called America's "romance," the belief that no one must aspire to be more, or endure to be less, than a citizen.

---

* For a similar view, see Steven Stark, "Populist Revolt," *Providence Phoenix*, 11 November 1994, 12.

Notes

1. A.G. Block, "The June Election: Dreadful Turnout Marks the 1994 Primary," *California Journal,* June 1994, 7; the vote against public bonds is reported in the same issue of the *California Journal,* p. 18.

2. Thomas B. Edsall, "The Politics of Fear," *Washington Post National Weekly,* 6–12 December 1993, 23.

3. James MacGregor Burns, *Roosevelt: The Lion and the Fox* (New York: Harcourt, Brace, 1956), esp. 318–19.

4. Adam Clymer, "The Hidden Antagonist of Clinton's Health Plan," *New York Times,* 19 June 1994, E1.

5. Frank and Cook are cited in Peter Passell, "Life's Hard? Blame the Markets," *New York Times,* 8 May 1994, E3.

6. Hobart Rowen, "Putting People to Work," *Washington Post National Weekly,* 24–30 May 1993, 5.

7. Hobart Rowen, "Our Own Worst Enemy," *Washington Post National Weekly,* 26 September–2 October 1994, 10.

8. E.J. Dionne, Jr., "New Democrat or Old Republican?" *Washington Post National Weekly,* 6–12 December 1993, 29; Thomas B. Edsall, "Clinton's Delicate Balancing Act," *Washington Post National Weekly,* 7–13 February 1994, 12.

9. Jason DeParle, "In Welfare Debate, It's Now Not 'How?' but 'Why?'" *New York Times,* 8 May 1994, E1.

10. Richard Berke, "The Tides That Brought Democrats to the GOP Have Turned," *New York Times,* 20 February 1994, E3.

11. Passell, "Life's Hard? Blame the Markets."

12. Richard Berke, "As Christians Pull GOP to the Right, Its Leaders Argue over Holding the Center," *New York Times,* 27 June 1994, A12.

13. E.J. Dionne, Jr., "Democratic Electorate Lacks Enthusiasm and Commitment," *Star-Ledger,* 30 June 1994, 23.

14. Martin Walker, "Bill Clinton's Secret Successes," *Washington Post National Weekly,* 12–18 September 1994, 23.

15. Jon Nordheimer, "Cuban Group Forges Link to Clinton," *New York Times,* 26 August 1994, A12.

16. *New York Times,* 21 August 1994, A35.

17. Howard Kurtz, "Once Over Easy on the Opposition," *Washington Post National Weekly,* 12–18 September 1994, 24.

18. *New York Times,* 21 August 1994, 35.

19. Norman Ornstein, "But Even in Congress, Money Can't Buy Everything," *Washington Post National Weekly,* 26 September–2 Octo-

ber 1994, 24.

20. Thomas Patterson, "Trust Politicians, Not the Press," *New York Times,* 15 December 1993, A27.

21. David Carlin, "It's the Culture, Stupid," *Commonweal,* 23 September 1994, 9–10.

22. See Louis Uchitelle's post-election analysis, "The Rise of the Losing Class," *New York Times,* 20 November 1994, E1.

23. *New York Times,* 10 November 1994, B15.

24. Richard Berke, "Where Did All the Issues Go?" *New York Times,* 23 October 1994, E1.

25. *New York Times,* 10 November 1994, B4.

26. *New York Times*/CBS Poll, 29 October–1 November 1994 .

Index

Index

"The President's Club," 45
Democrats and Democratic Party: assets of, 187–88; "big government" of, 54 55; Catholics and, 85 87; as champions of community, 96–97; and "civic ethic," 124; after Civil War, 8; conflict within, 163; defeats of, 83; elitist strain in, 199; for government intervention, 21; historic, 83–88; individualistic liberalism of, 87–88; necessity of, 45–49; and need for toughness, 133–34; 1984 congressional victories of, 65; 1984 prospects of, 77–78; 1988 campaign issues of, 117; and nominations, 114–15; and party loyalty, 80; quality candidates of, 184; and race as social issue, 164–66; victories of, 83; waning influence of, in South, 101–2
Dewey, Thomas E., 39
Dionne, E.J., Jr., 152, 170–71
Disaffiliation, public mood of, 153
Divided government, 153–54. *See also* Government
Dixiecrats, 79
Docudrama, 158
Dole, Robert, 21, 189
Dollar, decline in value of, 188
Dukakis, Michael: appeal of, 101–2; and Boston-Austin axis, 168; and Bush, 107–8, 118–19; on competence, 122, 167; liberalism of, 117; need of, for vision of future, 117–18; primary achievement of, 111–13; as soft on crime, 104, 120; on tax evaders, 130; vagueness of, 122; vulnerability of, 112

Economic concerns, importance of, 124–27
Economic disorder, and American civil order, 145–50

Economic expansion, current, 193–94
Economic growth, as standard of public policy, 187
Economic issue, in 1992, 146–47
Economic Report to the President (1991), 146–47
Economics, liberalism, politics, and, 119–27
Election of 1976: and American tradition, 27–29; and the economy, 21–24
Election of 1984, symbolism of, 97
Election of 1992, geography of, 169
Election of 1994, 11; messages of, 195–98
Elections, 2–3
Electorate: demobilization of, 105–6; nationalization of, 105
"Electronic town hall," 158
Employment, as prerequisite of social dignity, 95–96
Enterprise zones, 56
Equality: and equal rights, 172; and equal standards, 173
Equal justice, as Democratic pledge, 135–36
"Equivalence theorem," 151
Ethnic voters, appeals to, 87–88
Evangelical religion, effect of, on Democratic Party, 89–90. *See also* Born-again Christians; Religious right
"Expressive individualism," 129–30

Fairness Commission, 78
Fairness issue, defined, 84
Falwell, Jerry, 84
Family values, 170; deterioration of, 148; lack of standards for, 91–92
Fazio, Vic, 189
Federal government. *See* Government
Federal Reserve, role of, 150
Feinstein, Dianne, 184, 196, 199

About the Author

Wilson Carey McWilliams was born in California and grew up talking politics; his father was Carey McWilliams, the premier analyst of California politics and the long-time editor of *The Nation.*

He attended the University of California, Berkeley, where he received his Ph.D. in political science. He has taught at Oberlin College and Brooklyn College and, since 1970, has been professor of political science at Rutgers University, specializing in American politics and political thought, as well as religion and politics.

His writings include *The Idea of Fraternity in America*, which won the National Historical Society prize in 1973, in addition, he is a frequent contributor to *Commonweal* and other journals of opinion.

He has served as secretary and vice-president of the American Political Science Association and received the John Witherspoon Award for distinguished service to the humanities.